BRAIN GAMES™

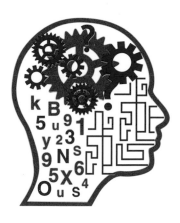

Consultant: Elkhonon Goldberg, Ph.D.

Publications International, Ltd

Elkhonon Goldberg, Ph.D., ABPP/ABCN, (consultant) is a clinical professor of neurology at New York University School of Medicine, a diplomate of the American Board of Professional Psychology/American Board of Clinical Neuropsychology, and director of The East-West Science and Education Foundation. Dr. Goldberg created the Manhattan-based Cognitive Enhancement Program, a fitness center for the brain, and he is author of the international best-selling books *The Wisdom Paradox: How Your Mind Can Grow as Your Brain Grows Older* and *The Executive Brain: Frontal Lobes and the Civilized Mind.*

Contributing Writers: Elkhonon Goldberg, Ph.D., Holli Fort

Puzzle Constructors: Cihan Altay, David L. Brown, Myles Callum, Philip Carter, © Clarity Media Ltd., Kelly Clark, Barry Clarke, Jeanette Dall, Mark Danna, Colin Edelman, Josie Faulkner, Adrian Fisher, Ray Hamel, Luke Haward, Shelly Hazard, Marilynn Huret, Lloyd King, Colleen Meinking, Dan Meinking, David Millar, Elsa Neal, Ellen F. Pill, Ph.D., Dave Roberts, Marylin Roberts, Stephen Ryder, Pete Sarjeant, Steve Schaefer, Paul Seaburn, Fraser Simpson, Terry Stickels, Howard Tomlinson

Additional Puzzle Editing: Fraser Simpson

Illustrators: Myles Callum, Dave Roberts, Marylin Roberts, Shavan R. Spears

CONTENTS

BRAIN FITNESS

Your mind is your most important asset—more important than your house, your bank account, and your stock portfolio. You insure your house and work hard to pad your bank account. But what can you do to sharpen your mind and protect it from decline? With the baby boomers getting on in years, an increasing number of people are asking this question. Modern-day science provides a clear answer: You can safeguard your mind by protecting your brain. To understand this relationship further, we turn to cutting-edge research.

Protect and Enhance Your Brainpower

Modern-day neuroscience has established that our brain is a far more plastic organ than was previously thought. In the past it was believed that an adult brain can only lose nerve cells (neurons) and cannot acquire new ones. Today we know that new neurons—and new connections between neurons—continue to develop throughout our lives, even well into advanced age. This process is called *neuroplasticity*. Thanks to recent scientific discoveries, we also know that we can harness the powers of neuroplasticity in protecting and even enhancing our minds at every stage of life—including our advanced years.

How can we harness neuroplasticity to help protect and enhance our mental powers? Recent scientific research demonstrates that the brain responds to mental stimulation much like muscles respond to physical exercise. In other words, you have to give your brain a workout. The more vigorous and diverse your mental life—and the more you welcome mental challenges—the more you will stimulate the growth of new neurons and new connections between them. Furthermore, the *nature* of your mental activities influences *where* in the brain this growth takes place. The brain is a very complex organ with different parts in charge of different mental functions. Thus, different cognitive challenges exercise different components of the brain.

How do we know this? We've learned this by combining experiments created from real-life circumstances with *neuroimaging*, the high-resolution technologies that allow scientists to study brain structure and function with amazing precision. Some say that these technologies have done for our understanding of the brain what the invention of the telescope has done for our understanding of the planetary systems. Thanks to these technologies, particularly MRI (magnetic resonance imaging), we know that certain parts of the brain exhibit an increased size in those who use these parts of the brain more than most people. For example, researchers found that the hippocampus, the part of the brain critical for spatial memory, was larger than usual in London cab drivers, who have to navigate and remember complex routes in a huge city. Studies revealed that the so-called Heschl's gyrus, a part of the temporal lobe of the brain involved in processing music, is larger in professional musicians than in musically untrained people. And the angular gyrus, the part of the brain involved in language, proved to be larger in bilingual individuals than in those who speak only one language.

What is particularly important is that the size of the effect—the extent to which a specific area of the brain was enlarged—was directly related to the  *amount of time* each person spent on activities that rely on that brain area. For instance, the hippocampal size was directly related to the number of years the cab driver spent on the job, and the size of Heschl's gyrus was associated with the amount of time a musician devoted to practicing a musical instrument. This shows that cognitive activity directly influences the structures of the brain by stimulating the effects of neuroplasticity in these structures, since the enlargement of brain regions implies a greater-than-usual number of cells or connections between them. The impact of cognitive activity on the brain can be great enough to result in an actual increase in its size! Indeed, different parts of the brain benefit directly from certain activities, and the effect can be quite specific.

Diversify Your Mental Workout

It is also true that any relatively complex cognitive function—be it memory, attention, perception, decision making, or problem solving—relies on a whole network of brain regions rather than on a single region. Therefore, any relatively complex mental challenge will engage more than one part of the brain. Yet no single mental activity will engage the whole brain.

This is why the diversity of your mental life is key to your overall brain health. The more vigorous and varied your cognitive challenges, the more efficiently and effectively they'll protect your mind from decline. To return to the workout analogy: Imagine a physical gym. No single exercise machine will make you physically fit. Instead, you need a balanced and diverse workout regimen.

You have probably always assumed that crossword puzzles and sudoku are good for you, and they are. But your cognitive workout will benefit more from a greater variety of exercises, particularly if these exercises have been selected with some knowledge of how the brain works.

The puzzle selection for *Brain Games*™ has been guided by these considerations—with knowledge of the brain and the roles played by its different parts in the overall orchestra of your mental life. We aimed to assemble as wide a range of puzzles as possible in order to offer the brain a full workout.

There is no single magic pill to protect or enhance your mind, but vigorous, regular, and diverse mental activity is the closest thing to it. Research indicates that people engaged in mental activities as a result of their education and vocation are less likely to develop dementia as they age. In fact, many of these people demonstrate impressive mental alertness well into their eighties and nineties.

What's more, this "magic pill" need not be bitter. You can engage in activities that are both good for your brain *and* fun. Different kinds of puzzles engage different aspects of your mind, and you can assemble them all into a cognitive workout regimen.

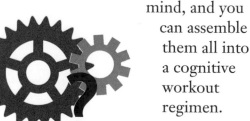

Variety is the name of the game—that's the whole idea! In each cognitive workout session, have fun by mixing puzzles of different kinds. This book offers you enough puzzle variety to make this possible.

When it comes to difficulty level, welcome challenging puzzles. Don't assume they're beyond your ability without giving them your best shot first. To be effective as a mental workout, the puzzles you choose should not be too easy or too difficult. An overly easy puzzle will not stimulate your brain, just as a leisurely walk in the park is not an efficient way to condition your heart. You need mental exertion. On the other hand, an overly difficult puzzle will just frustrate and discourage you from moving forward. So it is important to find the "challenge zone" that is appropriate for you. This may vary from person to person and from puzzle type to puzzle type. Here, too, the gym analogy applies. Different people will benefit most from different exercise machines and weight levels.

So we have tried to offer a range of difficulty for the various puzzle types. Try different puzzles to find the starting level appropriate for you. Soon, your puzzle-cracking ability will improve, and you may find that puzzles you once found too hard are now within your grasp.

Have Fun While Stretching Your Mind

The important thing is to have fun while doing something good for you. Puzzles can be engaging, absorbing, and even addictive. An increasing number of people make regular physical exercise part of their daily routines and miss it when circumstances prevent them from exercising. These habitual gym-goers know that strenuous effort is something to look forward to, not to avoid. Similarly, you will strengthen your mental muscle by actively challenging it. Don't put the puzzle book down when the solution is not immediately apparent. By testing your mind you will discover the joy of a particular kind of accomplishment: watching your mental powers grow. You must have the feeling of mental effort and exertion in order to exercise your brain.

This brings us to the next issue. While all puzzles are good for you, the degree of their effectiveness as brain conditioners is not the same. Some puzzles only test your knowledge of facts. Such puzzles may be enjoyable and useful to a degree, but they're not as useful in conditioning your brain as are the puzzles that require you to transform and manipulate information or do something with it by logic, multistep inference, mental rotation, planning, and so on. These latter puzzles are more likely to give you the feeling of mental exertion, of "stretching your mind," and they are also better for your brain health. You can use this feeling as a useful, though inexact, assessment of a puzzle's effectiveness as a brain conditioner.

Try to select puzzles in a way that complements, rather than duplicates, your job-related activities. If your profession involves dealing with words (e.g., an English teacher), try to emphasize spatial puzzles. If you are an engineer dealing with diagrams, focus on verbal puzzles. If your job is relatively devoid of mental challenges of any kind, mix several types of puzzles in equal proportions.

Cognitive decline frequently sets in with aging. It often affects certain kinds of memory and certain aspects of attention and decision making. So as you age, it is particularly important to introduce cognitive exercise into your lifestyle to counteract any possible cognitive decline. But cognitive exercise is also important for the young and the middle-aged. We live in a world that depends increasingly on the brain more than on brawn. It is important to be sharp in order to get ahead in your career and to remain at the top of your game.

How frequently should you exercise your mind and for how long? Think in terms of an ongoing lifestyle change and not just a short-term commitment. Regularity is key, perhaps a few times a week for 30 to 45 minutes at a time. We've tried to make this easier by offering a whole series of *Brain Games*™ books. You can carry one of these these puzzle books—your "cognitive workout gym"—in your briefcase, backpack, or shopping bag. Our puzzles are intended to be fun, so feel free to fit them into your lifestyle in a way that enhances rather than disrupts it. Research shows that even a relatively brief regimen of vigorous cognitive activity often produces perceptible and lasting effects. But as with physical exercise, the results are best when cognitive exercise becomes a lifelong habit.

To help you gauge your progress, we have included two self-assessment questionnaires: one near the beginning of the book and one near the end. The questionnaires will guide you in rating your cognitive abilities and any changes that you may experience as a result of doing puzzles. Try to be as objective as possible

when you fill out the questionnaires. Improving your cognitive skills in real-life situations is the most important practical outcome of exercising your mind, and you are in the best position to note whether and to what extent any improvement has taken place.

Now that you're aware of the great mental workout that awaits you in this book, we hope that you'll approach these puzzles with a sense of fun. If you have always been a puzzle fan, we offer a great rationale for indulging your passion! You have not been wasting your time by cracking challenging puzzles. Far from it! You have been training and improving your mind.

So, whether you are a new or seasoned puzzle-solver, enjoy your brain workout and get smarter as you go!

ASSESS YOUR BRAIN

You are about to do something very smart: embark on a set of exercises to improve the way your mind works. The puzzles assembled in this book are fun and they have been selected to hone your memory, attention, problem solving and other important mental skills. So before you begin, we would like you to fill out a brief questionnaire. It is for your own benefit, so you know how your mind worked before you challenged it with our exercises. This will allow you to decide in the future if any change in your mental performance has taken place, and in what areas.

The questions below are designed to test your skills in the areas of memory, problem solving, creative thinking, attention, language, and more. Please take a moment to think about your answers and rate your responses on a 5-point scale where 5 equals "excellent" and 1 equals "very poor." Then tally up your scores and go to the categories at the bottom of the page to see how you did.

1. You get a new cell phone. How long does it take you to remember the number? Give yourself a 1 if you have to check the phone every time you want to give out the number, and a 5 if you know it by heart the next day.

   1   2   3   4   5

2. How good are you at remembering where you put things? Give yourself a 5 if you never lose anything, but a 1 if you have to search for the keys every time you want to leave the house.

   1   2   3   4   5

3. You have a busy work day that you've carefully planned around a doctor's appointment. At the last minute, the doctor's office calls and asks you to reschedule your appointment from afternoon to morning. How good are you at juggling your plans to accommodate this change?

   1   2   3   4   5

4. You're taking a trip back to your hometown, and you have several old friends to see, as well as old haunts to visit. You'll only be there for three days. How good are you at planning your visit so you can accomplish everything?

   1   2   3   4   5

5. A friend takes you to the opera, and the next morning a curious coworker wants to hear the plot in depth. How good are you at remembering all the details?

   1   2   3   4   5

6. You're brokering an agreement between two parties, and each party keeps changing their demands. How good are you at adapting to the changing situation?

   1   2   3   4   5

7. You're cooking a big meal for a family celebration. You have to cook everything—appetizers, entrees, sides, and desserts—all on the same day. How good are you at planning out each recipe so that everything is done and you can sit down and enjoy the meal with your family?

1   2   3   4   5

8. In an emotionally charged situation (for example, when you're giving a toast), can you usually come up with the right words to describe your feelings?

1   2   3   4   5

9. You and five friends have made a vow to always spend a certain amount of money on each other for holiday gifts. How good are you at calculating the prices of things in your head to make sure you spend the right amount of money?

1   2   3   4   5

10. You're moving, and you have to coordinate all the details of packing, hiring movers, cutting off and setting up utilities, and a hundred other small details. How good are you at planning out this complex situation?

1   2   3   4   5

10–25 Points:
Are You Ready to Make a Change?

Remember, it's never too late to improve your brain health! A great way to start is to work puzzles each day, and you've taken the first step by buying this book. Choose a different type of puzzle each day, or do a variety of them to help strengthen memory, focus attention, and improve logic and problem solving.

26–40 Points:
Building Your Mental Muscles

You're no mental slouch, but there's always room to sharpen your mind! Choose puzzles that will challenge you, especially the types of puzzles you might not like as much or wouldn't normally do. Remember, doing a puzzle can be the mental equivalent of doing lunges or squats: While they might not be your first choice of activities, you'll definitely like the results!

41–50 Points:
View from the Top

Congratulations! You're keeping your brain in tip-top shape. To maintain this level of mental fitness, keep challenging yourself by working puzzles every day. Like the rest of the body's muscles, your mental strength can decline if you don't use it. So choose to keep your brain supple and strong. You're at the summit, now you just have to stay to enjoy the view!

Sudoku

LOGIC

		3		6				4
	6		3	4		5		1
	8			9	5			
3	5	1	9	7				
6			5		2			9
			1	8	6	5	3	
		6	2				3	
9		5		8	4		6	
4				5		8		

Use deductive logic to complete the grid so that each row, each column, and each 3 by 3 box contains the numbers 1 through 9 in some order. The solution is unique.

Go Figure

COMPUTATION **LOGIC**

Fill each square in the grid with a digit from 1 through 6. When the numbers in each row are multiplied, you should arrive at the total in the right-hand column. When the numbers in each column are multiplied, you should arrive at the total on the bottom line. The numbers in each corner-to-corner diagonal must multiply to the totals in the upper- and lower-right corners.

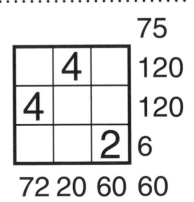

75

	4		120
4			120
		2	6

72 20 60 60

Answers on page 169.

A Matter of Time

ACROSS

1. Ralph of "The Waltons"
6. Chef's meas.
9. Dunderhead
12. Incorporate, as into a city
13. DDT-banning org.
14. Health-care grp.
15. Word after rubber or food
16. Giving more lip
18. Kind of timing
20. Suppresses
22. Cow's comment
23. Alliance formed in 1860 (abbr.)
24. Freezing cold
26. Wander
30. Current
34. Color changer
35. Took the gold medal
36. Some plasma screens
37. Gas price-watching org.
40. Beat badly
42. Noon
46. Google is a major one

47. Presses
50. _____ whim
51. Unprocessed
52. Fry in a pan
53. Muddy home
54. Ambulance destinations (abbr.)
55. Vote in, as a president

DOWN

1. "Able _____ I ere I…"
2. Uninvited picnic guest
3. On pins and needles
4. Part-time workers
5. Heroic act
6. It may require writing an essay
7. Uncontrollable muscle action
8. A slow stroll, perhaps in Spain
9. Where Dayton is
10. Interjection of agreement
11. Edsel maker
17. Treat with contempt
19. One-twelfth of a foot
20. Iraqi missile
21. "_____ with my little eye…"
25. Archery bow wood
27. Win a debate
28. Rugged roadsters (abbr.)
29. Netting
31. Doctorate hurdle

32. Nighttime flier
33. Not farmed out
38. Burning up
39. Rosy perfume
41. Living on a farm, perhaps
42. The terrible _____
43. Left
44. Cyberspace auction site
45. Conforms strictly
48. Truncation abbreviation
49. Arranged

Answers on page 169.

Hinky Pinky

The clues below lead to a 2-word answer that rhymes, such as Big Pig or Stable Table. The numbers in parentheses after the clue give the number of syllables in each word.

1. "The Raven" author's garden-watering tube (1): _____

2. Unclothed beneficiary of a will (1): _____

3. Scatterbrain throws in the towel (1): _____

4. Approaching an open space in a forest (2): _____

5. Very infrequent occurrence at an alms-giving organization (3): _____

Wacky Wordy

Can you "read" the phrase below?

P P P P P P

A A A A A A

C C C C C

K K K K K K

Answers on page 169.

Go Figure

9	6	2			3		28
	2	2		1			25
	7		2		4		21
2		9	5	3			25
1		2	5	4	2		24
	1		4	8	3		21
							27
26	27	26	21	23	20	29	

Fill each square in the grid with a digit from 1 through 9. When the numbers in each row are added, you should arrive at the total in the right-hand column. When the numbers in each column are added, you should arrive at the total on the bottom line. The numbers in each corner-to-corner diagonal must add up to the totals in the upper- and lower-right corners.

But Who Controlled the Radio?

As usual, John refused to look at a map or ask for directions when he and his wife, Marsha, went on a road trip. By sheer luck, they managed to take the same route both ways. John was driving when they left the house, but Marsha drove the last 65 miles. On the way back, John drove the first 50 miles, then Marsha sat behind the wheel the rest of the way. Marsha swears she drove more miles than John, but without a map she thinks she has no proof. Is Marsha right?

Answers on page 169.

Acrostic Clues

Solve the clues below and then place the letters in their corresponding spots in the grid to reveal a historic quote. The letter in the upper-right corner of each grid square refers to the clue the letter comes from.

1 C	2 A	3 D	4 I		5 A	6 H	7 A		8 J	9 G	10 J	11 C	12 C		13 K	14 A
15 C	16 E	17 G		18 I	19 D	20 G	21 D	22 A	23 B	24 A	25 F	26 G		27 D	28 E	
29 E	30 I	31 B	32 K	33 F	34 E	35 F	36 E		37 G	38 J	39 I		40 H	41 A	42 A	43 A
44 G	45 H	46 A	47 H	48 D	49 I		50 A	51 J		52 J	53 G	54 B	55 C	56 E	57 B	58 K
59 G	60 G	61 H	62 K	63 J		64 E	65 D	66 I		67 E	68 F	69 E	70 K	71 B	72 E	73 G

A. Author of quote (2 words)

— — — — — — — — — — —
(43) (2) (50) (5) (46) (42) (14) (41) (22) (7) (24)

B. Surprise football tactic

— — — — —
(54) (23) (31) (57) (71)

C. Resided

— — — — —
(12) (1) (55) (11) (15)

D. 31st U.S. President (1929–1933)

— — — — — —
(65) (27) (48) (21) (3) (19)

E. Candid and straight to the point

— — — — — — — — — —
(28) (72) (56) (64) (67) (69) (34) (36) (16) (29)

F. "King _____" (1933)

— — — —
(33) (68) (35) (25)

G. Unfair circumstances

— — — — — — — — — —
(20) (73) (17) (59) (60) (9) (37) (53) (26) (44)

H. Metropolis of northern India

— — — — —
(47) (6) (40) (45) (61)

I. Sister's son

— — — — — —
(4) (39) (18) (30) (66) (49)

J. Corpulent

— — — — — —
(51) (52) (10) (63) (38) (8)

K. State of agreement

— — — — —
(13) (32) (70) (62) (58)

Answers on page 169.

Football Fever
by Alpha Sleuth™

Move each of the letters below into the grid to form common words. You will use each letter only once. The letters in the numbered cells of the grid correspond to the letters in the phrase below the grid. Completing the grid will help you complete the phrase, and vice versa. When finished, the grid and phrase should be filled with valid words, and you will have used all the letters in the letter set. The letters already included in the grid will help get you started.

HINT: The numbered cells in the grid are arranged alphabetically, so the letter in the cell marked 1 will appear in the alphabet before the letter in the cell marked 2, and so on.

A B C D E F G H I J K L M N
O P Q R S T U V W X Y Z

9	4	3	10	5	4	7

9	6	1	11	8	2	2

Versatile Verbiage

One 4-letter word can be placed after each word below to form a new word or phrase. What's the all-purpose word?

BIG, ELASTIC, HEAD, SWEAT

Answers on pages 169–170.

Word Jigsaw

LANGUAGE SPATIAL PLANNING

Fit the pieces into the frame to form common, uncapitalized words reading across and down crossword-style. There's no need to rotate the pieces; they'll fit as shown, with each piece used exactly once.

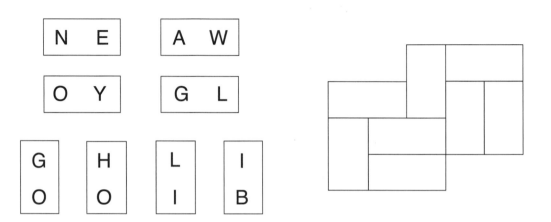

Word Ladder

LANGUAGE PLANNING

Change just one letter on each line to go from the top word to the bottom word. Do not change the order of the letters. You must have a word at each step.

MICE

‾‾‾‾

‾‾‾‾

‾‾‾‾

RATS

Answers on page 170.

Can You Be Picture-Perfect?

These 2 photos may look the same, but there are some subtle differences. Can you find all 4?

Answers on page 170.

Word Ladder

Change just one letter on each line to go from the top word to the bottom word. Do not change the order of the letters. You must have a word at each step.

TRUE

_____

_____

_____

_____

BLUE

Contain Yourself

For the clues below, you are looking for a small word that fits in a larger "container" word. For example, "vegetable in a weapon (3 letters in 5 letters)" would be s(pea)r.

Writing implement in a description of price (3 letters in 9 letters)

Satanic character in old-style theatrical entertainment (5 letters in 10 letters)

"Messiah" composer in overhead light fixture (6 letters in 10 letters)

Trivia on the Brain
Blueberries are currently hailed by scientists as a "super brain food" that can actually slow the aging process in your brain!

Answers on page 170.

Shrouded Summary

ATTENTION   GENERAL KNOWLEDGE   VISUAL SEARCH   LANGUAGE

Hidden in the word search below is a synopsis of a well-known story. The words you need to find are listed below, but in the word search they are presented in an order that will make a little more sense. The words may be vertical, horizontal, or diagonal. Can you name the story?

BEFORE

BUT

FAMILY

FINDING

FOR

GANG

HAS

HIDES

HIM

LEADER

ORPHAN

OTHER

OUT

PLANS

REAL

THIEVES

WITH

```
B O R P H A N I N P L T K W
H A H D I O T H W I H O P N
E F K J D L S N R E G G R N
N S Y S E R H Y M T B F I P
L T L H S O U T O T B H O W
O E O N W E A E V A U A R H
T I A I K I R I I A I N A K
P I B D H T T L T C E G I K
P H F I L H H H P S U A N V
R N A R N M I A R H M N C W
I Y L A R N E Q C R P O N S
O T L C A L V S N I B I O J
R E G O J B E F O R E N G M
A I A D L F S I I E K S T A
I M L I T L T N N A N I N C
Z C I Y D N E D G L J L P A
W Y W J T K I I F A M I L Y
F A P O S N C N B W N L E M
I D L F N T R G U P R H A S
H T R O T H E R T L S T D U
T U A R D A I E G A N G E F
D S I F G L F M A N I A R B
N W R A T V W L D S D G D L
```

Answers on page 170.

Find the Word

ATTENTION   LANGUAGE   VISUAL SEARCH

Ignoring spaces, capitalization, and punctuation, find all 22 occurrences of the consecutive letters D-O-G in the paragraph below.

Fred, ogre of the land of Prado Gamma, declared that the dogma of endogamy, requiring him to wed ogres only, was unfair. Fred doggedly courted Endogia, a lover of avocado gum, but not a weirdo girl. He wrote her doggerel, sent her hotdogs, and took her to a black tie dinner, but his tuxedo got caught on a nail, and everyone saw his Speedo garment underneath. Fred moped in his condo garage until Endogia's parents, after much ado, gave their permission to wed. Ogres from Prado Gamma thought the wedding was a boondoggle, and they were proven right when Fred ogled the maid of honor and Endogia said, "No can do—goodbye!"

Name Calling

ATTENTION   VISUAL SEARCH

Decipher the encoded word in the quip below using the numbers and letters on the phone pad. Remember that each number can stand for 3 or 4 possible letters.

Making 4–5–6–8–3–7 is a real hands-on experience.

1	2 ABC	3 DEF
4 GHI	5 JKL	6 MNO
7 PQRS	8 TUV	9 WXYZ
	0	

Answers on page 170.

Sudoku

Use deductive logic to complete the grid so that each row, each column, and each 3 by 3 box contains the numbers 1 through 9 in some order. The solution is unique.

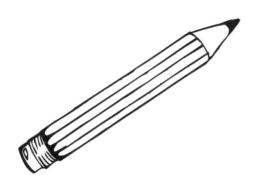

			9	1	8		6	2
		5		2	9		1	
	8		5			3		
	5			1		9		8
	6	2				7	5	
1		3		7			2	
		6			1		8	
	2		3	4		1		
5	1			9	8	6		

Three of a Kind

Fill in the blanks in the sentences below with 3-letter words that are anagrams (rearrangements of the same letters) of one another.

Dad hurt his _____ when the big _____ knocked him into the fence.

The Queen said, " I _____ thee Sir _____."

I felt a little _____ when the _____ stuck my finger.

My pet _____ didn't _____ normally.

The wall looked _____ with the _____ of dirt on it.

Answers on page 170.

Snack Attack

The man in the upper-right corner with the snacks needs a little assistance avoiding obstacles so he can get back to his seat in the bleachers and enjoy the game. Can you help him?

Answer on page 171.

Go Figure

COMPUTATION   LOGIC

Fill each square in the grid with a digit from 1 through 9. When the numbers in each row are added, you should arrive at the total in the right-hand column. When the numbers in each column are added, you should arrive at the total on the bottom line. The numbers in each corner-to-corner diagonal must add up to the totals in the upper- and lower-right corners.

							29
6		4	9		2		27
	4	3					23
2		7	1	6	4		22
1	6			5			27
	9		3	3	1		28
7		3	4	4	5		27
27	30	26	26	24	21	32

Hinky Pinky

GENERAL KNOWLEDGE   LANGUAGE

The clues below lead to a 2-word answer that rhymes, such as Big Pig or Stable Table. The numbers in parentheses after the clue give the number of syllables in each word. This particular puzzle has a double theme.

1. Tidy putting area (1): _____

2. Frigid precious metal (1): _____

3. Selected an American Beauty (1): _____

4. Quote "Wheel of Fortune" star Vanna (1): _____

5. Make "The DaVinci Code" author Dan king (1): _____

The double theme is: _____

Answers on page 171.

Explore Your Mind

ACROSS

1. Oil market cartel (abbr.)
5. Maker of pens and lighters
8. Use an ax
12. Part of the foot
13. The end of an _____
14. Pushy and unfriendly
15. Leader of the first circumnavigation of the world
17. Prophetic sign
18. Feel poorly
19. Pull on a chain
21. First Spaniard to reach Florida
26. Minor slip
27. "_____ River Valley"
28. Temporary bed
30. "Let Us Now Praise Famous Men" writer James
31. Swindle
32. Simple, flowerless plant
33. Part of MPH
34. To's opposite
35. Salute with wine
36. He blazed the Wilderness Road into Kentucky
39. Popular hedging plant

40. Direction on a submarine
41. Economic gain
44. Leader of four expeditions to the New World
49. Old West lawman Wyatt
50. WWW address
51. Basic currency of Italy since 1999
52. Bridge shape
53. Some NFL linemen (abbr.)
54. Location of zip code 10001 (abbr.)

DOWN

1. Unit of electrical resistance
2. Toy shooter's ammo
3. Brain scan (abbr.)
4. Remove stains from
5. Heroine of Disney's "Beauty and the Beast"
6. "Rosemary's Baby" author Levin
7. Military snack bar
8. Oscar winner Russell
9. Drone
10. Poem of praise
11. Write
16. Biting insects
20. Advanced in age
21. Flipped through a book
22. Coloratura's genre
23. Slobber
24. View from the coast
25. Like the Vikings
26. Once around the track

29. High explosive
31. Short hairdo
32. They accompanied Cinderella to the ball
34. Expression of disapproval
35. Vegetarian's protein source
37. Beautiful maiden
38. Snooker targets
41. "Petticoat Junction" star Benaderet
42. Sculling need
43. Tolkien creature
45. Mine output
46. Purchase
47. Coffee dispenser
48. _____ sauce

Answers on page 171.

Animal House

Four animals have to pay their rent, but the landlord cannot remember in what order they usually pay. He also has their details mixed up in his notebook. Although each item appears in the correct column, only one item in each column is cor-

	Name	Animal	Location
1	Andy	elephant	cave
2	Brenda	flamingo	field
3	Clive	goat	shed
4	Dolly	horse	wood

rectly positioned. The following facts are true about the correct order:

1. The animal named Dolly is either the flamingo or the elephant, and her location is either the field or shed.

2. Neither the cave nor the field is second.

3. Either Andy or Dolly lived in either the wood or the field, and the item directly above is neither Brenda nor Dolly and is either the goat or elephant.

4. Either Brenda or Dolly is first.

5. Neither the goat nor the elephant is third.

6. The horse is not last.

Can you determine the correct name, animal, and location for each position?

Anagrams at Work

Fill in the blanks in the sentence below with 7-letter words that are anagrams (rearrangements of the same letters) of one another.

The 4-star _____ asked his assistant to _____ the photograph so he could get a closer view of the intended target.

Answers on page 171.

Code-Doku

Use deductive logic to complete the grid so that each row, each column, and each 3 by 3 box contains the letters in the words WASN'T HELD. When you have completed the puzzle, read the shaded squares to see a traditional saying.

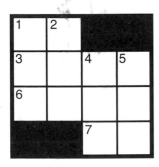

T	D		H	W				E
		H			A			
S					D		N	
N			D					
					H			N
		E		A	L		T	
			A			H		
		T					A	
E	H					W	S	D

Number Crossword

Fill in this crossword with numbers instead of letters. Use the clues to determine which number from 1 through 9 belongs in each empty square. No zeros are used.

ACROSS
1. A multiple of 9
3. Consecutive digits, ascending
6. Consecutive digits, ascending
7. A multiple of 11

DOWN
1. A palindrome
2. Three different digits
4. Three different digits
5. Consecutive even digits, ascending

Answers on page 171.

Word Columns

LANGUAGE PLANNING SPATIAL REASONING

Find the hidden phrase by using the letters directly below each of the blank squares. Each letter is used only once.

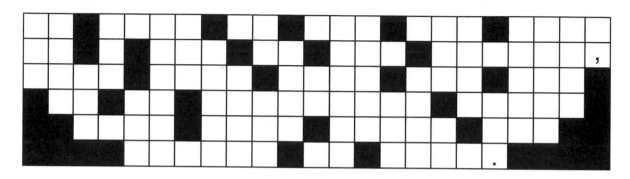

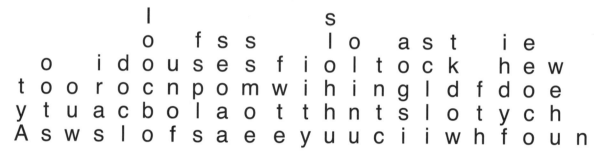

```
                    l                       s
              o       f   s   s       l   o   a   s   t       i   e
      o       i   d   o   u   s   e   s   f   i   o   l   t   o   c   k       h   e   w
  t   o   o   r   o   c   n   p   o   m   w   i   h   i   n   g   l   d   f   d   o   e
  y   t   u   a   c   b   o   l   a   o   t   t   h   n   t   s   l   o   t   y   c   h
  A   s   w   s   l   o   f   s   a   e   e   y   u   u   c   i   i   w   h   f   o   u   n
```

Trivia on the Brain

Contrary to popular belief, yawning doesn't mean that you're sleepy—or that your brain lacks oxygen, as some studies have suggested. Yawning is actually a cooling mechanism for your brain that increases blood flow and brings cool air with it—keeping your brain from overheating!

Answers on page 172.

A Real Cakewalk

Picture this maze as a tasty cake. Your goal is the same as for any baked good—get from the outside to the center as quickly as possible, but don't slip on the frosting!

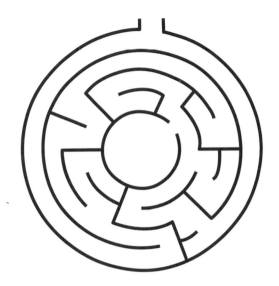

Word Ladder

Change just one letter on each line to go from the top word to the bottom word. Do not change the order of the letters. You must have a word at each step.

CORK

____

____

____

WINE

Answers on page 172.

Sudoku

Use deductive logic to complete the grid so that each row, each column, and each 3 by 3 box contains the numbers 1 through 9 in some order. The solution is unique.

		7			3	5		4
4			9		1			
3	8	9				6		
9		2	5			7	8	1
	7						6	
6	5	8			4	2		9
		1				9	4	6
			1		9			2
5		4	2		1			

Fitting Words

In this miniature crossword, the clues are listed randomly and are numbered for convenience only. It is up to you to figure out the placement of the 9 answers. To help you out, we've inserted one letter in the grid, and this is the only occurrence of that letter in the puzzle.

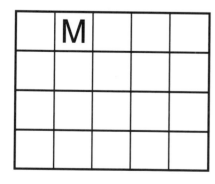

CLUES

1. Simple
2. Does pressing work
3. Packed with the latest information
4. Forehead
5. Related (to)
6. Stroll
7. Oliver Twist's request
8. "M*A*S*H" setting
9. Microscope part

Answers on page 172.

Letterbox Passport

The letters in the country QATAR can be found in boxes 5, 8, 10, and 16, but not necessarily in that order. Similarly, the letters in all the other country names below can be found in the boxes indicated. Insert all the letters of the alphabet into the boxes; if you do this correctly, the shaded cells will reveal another nation.

Hint: Look for names that share a single letter. For example, PERU shares a P with JAPAN and an R with QATAR. By comparing the number lists, you can then deduce the values of these letters.

1	2	3	4	5	6	7	8	9	10	11	12	13

14	15	16	17	18	19	20	21	22	23	24	25	26

BELGIUM: 1, 4, 7, 9, 18, 23, 24

CHILE: 4, 7, 9, 13, 21

DENMARK: 7, 8, 10, 11, 12, 17, 24

FRANCE: 7, 8, 10, 11, 21, 26

GERMANY: 1, 7, 8, 10, 11, 15, 24

HOLLAND: 9, 10, 11, 12, 13, 25

JAPAN: 10, 11, 14, 19

KUWAIT: 3, 4, 5, 10, 17, 18

LATVIA: 4, 5, 9, 10, 22

MEXICO: 4, 7, 20, 21, 24, 25

PERU: 7, 8, 14, 18

QATAR: 5, 8, 10, 16

SWEDEN: 2, 3, 7, 11, 12

ZIMBABWE: 3, 4, 6, 7, 10, 23, 24

Answers on page 172.

Word Jigsaw

Fit the pieces into the frame to form common, uncapitalized words reading across and down crossword-style. There's no need to rotate the pieces; they'll fit as shown, with each piece used exactly once.

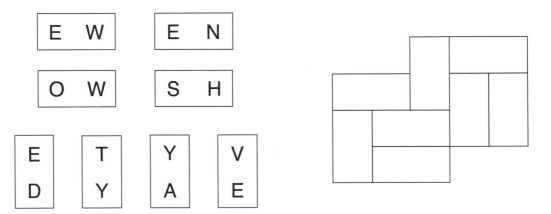

A Whale of a Challenge

While in pursuit of plankton, this whale went to pieces. Can you put him back together mentally? The pieces haven't been flipped or rotated.

Answers on page 172.

Army Show

The army entertainment troupe members have decided on the order their acts are to go on stage, but the stage manager has mixed up the order on his list. Although each item is in the correct column, only

	Title	Surname	Act
1	Private	Buckshot	comedy
2	Colonel	Trumpet	piano
3	Sergeant	Bark	acting
4	Major	Rattle	juggling

one item in each column is correctly positioned. The following facts are true about the correct order:

1. Private is not second.

2. Acting is one place below Bark.

3. Buckshot is not second.

4. Buckshot is one place above Major.

5. Colonel is one place below comedy.

6. Rattle is third.

Can you determine the title, surname, and act for each position?

Eight Is Enough

Fill in the blanks in the sentence below with 8-letter words that are anagrams (rearrangements of the same letters) of one another.

Although Al always looked for a silver lining in a bad situation, he could see only the _____ in getting left out of the will and being _____ by his parents.

Answers on page 172.

Acrostic Clues

Solve the clues below and then place the letters in their corresponding spots in the grid to reveal an inspirational quote. The letter in the upper-right corner of each grid square refers to the clue the letter comes from.

1 F	2 D	3 G	4 I	■	5 A	6 G	7 A	8 B	■	9 G	10 A	11 I	12 E	13 G	14 C	■	15 B	16 F
17 B	18 C	19 F	■	20 D	21 H	22 A	23 I	■	24 H	25 E	26 F	27 E	■	28 H	29 E	30 E	31 A	32 A	33 G
■	34 H	35 A	■	36 H	37 A	38 C	■	39 H	40 H	41 F	42 C	■	43 A	44 D	45 C	46 E	47 E	48 G	49 B
50 I	51 D	52 C	53 A	54 A	55 B	56 G	57 A	■	58 E	59 A	■	60 I	61 A	62 C	63 D
64 A	65 C	66 F	67 D	■	68 A	69 I	70 G	71 G	72 B	73 A	■	74 D	75 E

A. Author of quote (3 words)

— — — — — — — — — — — — — — — — — —
(32) (22) (5)(53)(61) (68) (54) (64) (57)(59) (7) (43) (10) (37) (35) (31)(73)

B. Largest country

— — — — — —
(55) (15) (49)(8) (72) (17)

C. Nobel's invention

— — — — — — — —
(14) (42) (18)(62)(52) (65) (45) (38)

D. Dud or failure

— — — — — — —
(20) (44) (67)(2) (51) (74) (63)

E. Takes the stand

— — — — — — — — —
(46) (29) (75)(58)(12) (30) (25) (47) (27)

F. Scandinavian country

— — — — — —
(16) (1) (26)(19)(66) (41)

G. Sleep through winter

— — — — — — — — — —
(71) (6) (9)(33)(48) (13) (3) (70) (56)

H. Large flatfish

— — — — — — — —
(21) (36) (24)(40)(28) (34) (39)

I. Jerk

— — — — — —
(23) (60) (69)(4) (50) (11)

Answers on page 172.

What's Wrong With This Picture?

This classroom is definitely crazy, but it's not just the kids who are out of control. There are 16 things wrong here that are helping to feed this room's 3 R's—rowdy, rambunctious, and ridiculous. Can you find them all?

Answers on page 172.

Wax On, Wax Off

ACROSS

1. Former transcontinental planes (abbr.)
5. Snoozes
9. 21st letter of the Greek alphabet
12. Gumbo vegetable
13. Leave out
14. German article
15. Illegal corn liquor
17. Took a stool
18. Republic in southeast Africa
19. Cauldron
21. Building extension
22. And others (abbr.)
24. Not as dark
25. Church structure
27. Proverbial lookalikes
28. Curry favor with
31. Let fall to the floor

32. Show again
33. Plentiful
35. Insecticide banned since 1973
36. X-ray alternative
39. Coral producers
41. Sure winner
43. Singer/actress Zadora
44. Wearing one's birthday suit
46. Show fallibility
47. "Goodbye, Sophia"
48. _____ Royale National Park
49. Object, in law
50. Pack away
51. Prophet

25. Make use of
26. "Antiques _____"
28. Movable cupboard
29. Columnar trees
30. Flexible
31. Well-dressed
34. Many Biblical films
36. Clock climber, in a nursery rhyme
37. Shoulder firearm
38. Suggest
40. State of irritation
42. Japanese sashes
45. Universal ideal

DOWN
1. French department or river
2. A toast to one's health
3. Wild-haired doll
4. Yemen's capital
5. Pitcher's dream game
6. French friend
7. Variety of champagne
8. Exorbitant, for a price
9. Grinding tools
10. Florida racetrack
11. Buries
16. Just peachy
20. Mammal with a long snout
23. Like a bullfighter

Answers on page 173.

Where We Live

Every word listed is contained within the box of letters below. The words can be found in a straight line horizontally, vertically, or diagonally. The words can be read backward or forward.

APARTMENT   MANSION

CASTLE   PALACE

CHALET   RANCH

COTTAGE   TENT

DUPLEX   TOWNHOUSE

FARMHOUSE   YURT

IGLOO

LODGE

```
T R U Y R A N C H E
N O I S N A M O S G
E L W M X T N U I A
M O E N N E O G D T
T D L E H H L Y A T
R G T N M O O P V O
A E S R O M U E U C
P P A L A C E S B D
A F C H A L E T E R
```

Name Calling

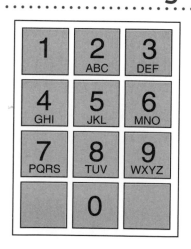

```
 1      2      3
       ABC    DEF

 4      5      6
GHI    JKL    MNO

 7      8      9
PQRS   TUV   WXYZ

        0
```

Decipher the encoded word in the quip below using the numbers and letters on the phone pad. Remember that each number can stand for 3 or 4 possible letters.

The most acute indigestion is often caused by the 9–6–7–3–7 we've eaten.

Answers on page 173.

Number Crossword

Fill in this crossword with numbers instead of letters. Use the clues to determine which number from 1 through 9 belongs in each empty square. No zeros are used.

ACROSS

1. An even number
4. Consecutive digits, ascending
6. Each of its digits (after the first one) is double the previous digit
7. An even number

DOWN

1. Consecutive digits out of order
2. A number of the form AABB
3. Consecutive digits, descending
5. A palindrome

Hinky Pinky

The clues below lead to a 2-word answer that rhymes, such as Big Pig or Stable Table. The numbers in parentheses after the clue give the number of syllables in each word.

1. Fast tongue action on an ice-cream cone (1): _____

2. Practical joke at a money-lending institution (1): _____

3. Philadelphia team player's Easter flowers (2): _____

4. Slender projectile shot from a bow (2): _____

5. TV game show group members' psychiatrists (3): _____

Answers on page 173.

GET YOUR MIND MOVING

Sudoku

LOGIC

		6		1	8			
5	6	8		7				1
	1		5	8				
6			1				9	2
		2			4			
8	9				4			6
				9	2		4	
	8			1		7	3	9
		5	7		6			

Use deductive logic to complete the grid so that each row, each column, and each 3 by 3 box contains the numbers 1 through 9 in some order. The solution is unique.

Powerful Anagrams

LANGUAGE

Fill in the blanks in the sentence below with 7-letter words that are anagrams (rearrangements of the same letters) of one another.

When the smoking volcano finally _____, the plume of ash was _____ to be the largest in Earth's history.

Answers on page 173.

A Puzzling Perspective

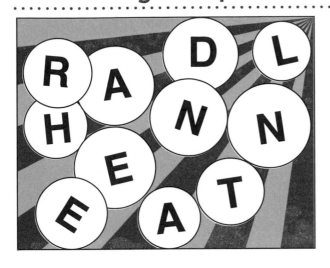

Mentally arrange the lettered balls from large to small in the correct order to spell an 11-letter word.

Clue: Extinct hominid

Word Ladder

Change just one letter on each line to go from the top word to the bottom word. Do not change the order of the letters. You must have a common English word at each step.

DAILY

_____

_____

_____

_____

_____

DOZEN

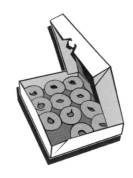

Answers on page 173.

Gesundheit! by Alpha Sleuth™

GENERAL KNOWLEDGE

LANGUAGE

PLANNING

Move each of the letters below into the grid to form common words. You will use each letter only once. The letters in the numbered cells of the grid correspond to the letters in the phrase below the grid. Completing the grid will help you complete the phrase, and vice versa. When finished, the grid and phrase should be filled with valid words, and you will have used all the letters in the letter set. The letters already included in the grid will help get you started.

HINT: The numbered cells in the grid are arranged alphabetically, so the letter in the cell marked 1 will appear in the alphabet before the letter in the cell marked 2, and so on.

A B C D E F G H I J K L
M N O P Q R S T U V W
X Y Z

Trivia on the Brain

During the late stages of pregnancy, the brains of expectant mothers have actually been shown to shrink. It can then take women's brains up to 6 months to regain their normal size!

Answers on page 173.

Fitting Words

LANGUAGE   LOGIC   PLANNING

In this miniature crossword, the clues are listed randomly and are numbered for convenience only. It is up to you to figure out the placement of the 9 answers. To help you out, we've inserted one letter in the grid, and this is the only occurrence of that letter in the puzzle.

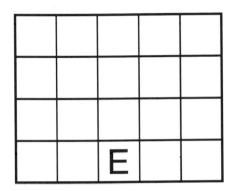

CLUES
1. Bards
2. Kind of sax
3. Hawaiian hello
4. "Follow _____ car!"
5. Paper nest builder
6. "Chopsticks" is one
7. Traditional knowledge
8. Hockey helmet feature
9. Microwaves

Sucker Bet

LOGIC

A local hustler at a bar in Atlantic City decided to take some money from the tourist sitting next to him. "See that couple over there?" he asked the guy. "They're married to each other, and their names are Vern and Shirley. I'll bet you $10 that Shirley has taken two trips to Atlantic City with her husband Vern, but Vern has only taken one trip to Atlantic City with his wife Shirley." The man thought this was impossible and took the bet. How did the hustler walk out of the bar with the visitor's sawbuck?

Answers on page 173.

Holy Isograms!

ATTENTION   LANGUAGE   VISUAL SEARCH

Our friend Buck Fitzgerald finds himself strangely drawn to isograms—words or phrases that have no repeating letters. Could that fascination have anything to do with his name? Help Buck feed his fascination by finding the 19 isograms in the grid of letters below. The words can be found in a straight line horizontally, vertically, or diagonally and may read backward or forward.

```
C S Q B A K I N G P O W D E R F R O D
E E Y J A C K I N T H E B O X Z S V Y
I E T I T O V D D N A L R E Z T I W S
S Y F U O H Z B Y U E N O Q F W N L O
A I A X L L G T L X G H T L G K T T U
B U D O H F R I I U B Z Y N R Y T X P
T H O Z Z T C C F E E I I N I X Y I K
N O R C Y L O I A D N M W U A Q M S I
U L P V A G M U G G R O O T H K F T T
O A S W R D T K S A G O H N E P Z R C
C K R A E Y Q A W L M P W A D P U A H
M J P T S K U E A M M A H S N A O E E
C H X H B C S D P S V C T Y O E Y H N
Y H O L E U I Z M P R H M Z L S O F I
Y P Z R O R Q F T V D Y T V B J X O C
M B B H B K J M X R H D M V G Z G G H
Z H U Q F C O R N F I E L D S J P N L
M O D E L T R A I N S R V X A A P I F
F X O Z V C V M H E R M A N W O U K P
```

BAKING POWDER	CORNFIELDS	JACK IN THE BOX	PACHYDERM
BEAUTY SHOP	COUNT BASIE	KING OF HEARTS	SOUP KITCHEN
BLONDE HAIR	FLYING SAUCER	LEXICOGRAPHY	SWITZERLAND
BLUE MONDAY	HERMAN WOUK	MAGIC FLUTE	SWORDFIGHT
BRIDAL GOWN	HOUSEWARMING	MODEL TRAINS	

Answers on page 174.

Go Figure

Fill each square in the grid with a digit from 1 through 6. When the numbers in each row are multiplied, you should arrive at the total in the right-hand column. When the numbers in each column are multiplied, you should arrive at the total on the bottom line. The numbers in each corner-to-corner diagonal must multiply to the totals in the upper- and lower-right corners.

				300
	4		3	144
1				40
		2		90
	1	2		32
24	40	120	144	32

Word Jigsaw

Fit the pieces into the frame to form common, uncapitalized words reading across and down crossword-style. There's no need to rotate the pieces; they'll fit as shown, with each piece used exactly once.

E	D

N	I

P	O

A	S

H
Y

C
T

G
R

U
B

Answers on page 174.

Bad Weather

ACROSS

1. Put into play
4. "_____ Blue" (TV show)
8. What a pumpkin grows on
12. Wrinkly dog
13. Honolulu's island
14. Wrinkle remover
15. San Diego Chargers logo
18. Go after
19. Golfer Els
20. Drilling site?
21. Ore tester
23. Hosp. trauma units
24. "_____ to Avoid" (1965 Herman's Hermits hit)
25. Weather protection at the entrance
29. Tiny amounts
30. Occult ability
33. Female grouse
36. Ipso _____
38. Actor Davis

39. Suit maker
40. Suddenly astonished
43. "When you get right down _____ ..."
44. Beef or pork
45. Location of UFO sightings
46. Sgt. Snorkel's dog
47. Nimble
48. Road twist

DOWN

1. Missing one's bedtime
2. One seeking a mate
3. Picnic contest
4. Tally mark
5. Pull quickly
6. Fraternity letter
7. Pester for payment
8. Violinist's asset
9. Subtle sarcasm
10. "It's the truth!"
11. Participate in
16. Cap
17. Painting surface
21. Jordan's capital
22. Brewskis
24. Comedian Johnson
26. Connect with
27. Partner of aahed
28. Howard Hughes became one

31. Part of a mutual fund
32. 1982 comedy about high schoolers
33. _____ voce
34. _____ in the dark
35. Astronaut's attire
36. Silent film comedian Arbuckle
37. Tire filler
39. Ruler mixed up in arts?
41. In typography-speak, more than one long dash
42. Account exec

Answers on page 174.

Take a Shot

Something about this spherical maze reminds us of a basketball. See if you can dribble your way from the entrance on the left side to the exit on the right side.

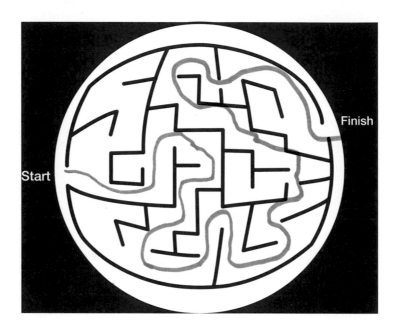

Number Square

GENERAL KNOWLEDGE   LOGIC

Each lettered box in the grid contains a number from 1 through 9. Use the clues to put the digits in their proper places. Each number is used only once.

A	B	C
D	E	F
G	H	I

CLUES

1. The top row contains only digits that are odd prime numbers
2. The middle row contains only digits that are square numbers
3. C + E = G
4. The digits A, F, B, and I are in consecutive order, ascending

Answers on page 174.

Code-Doku

Use deductive logic to complete the grid so that each row, each column, and each 3 by 3 box contains the letters in the words ICE TO MUSH. When you have completed the puzzle, read the shaded squares to form a twist on a traditional saying.

E			T		H	O		
	T			C	I			
		C					S	
	S				U		O	
					E	M		I
		I						
			E			I		
		E				S	U	
M				U	C			H

Name Calling

1	2 ABC	3 DEF
4 GHI	5 JKL	6 MNO
7 PQRS	8 TUV	9 WXYZ
	0	

Decipher the encoded word in the quip below using the numbers and letters on the phone pad. Remember that each number can stand for 3 or 4 possible letters.

8–4–2–8–6–7–9 goes to the player who makes the next-to-last mistake.

Answers on page 174.

What's Wrong With This Picture?

ATTENTION

So many people are talking about the 18 things wrong in this picture of a library that the librarian has lost control. Can you identify all the problems and help restore order?

Answers on page 174.

Newsroom Scramblegram

Four 8-letter words, all of which revolve around the same theme, have been jumbled. Unscramble the 4 words and write the answers in the space next to each one. Next, transfer the letters that are in the shaded boxes into the empty spaces below and unscramble the 9-letter word that goes with the theme. The theme for this puzzle is journalism.

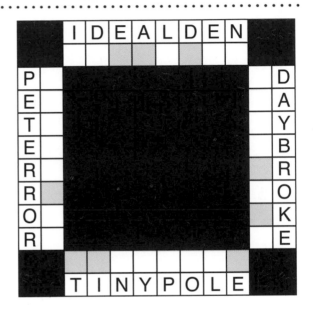

Contain Yourself

For the clue below, you are looking for a small word that fits in a larger "container" word. For example, "vegetable in a weapon (3 letters in 5 letters)" would be s(pea)r.

Roman emperor in benevolence (4 letters in 10 letters)

Answers on page 175.

Sudoku

2	3		7	1		5		
					6			
7		4			8	2		
			1					8
8		9		5		7		4
3				4				
		6	3			4		5
			2					
		7		6	5		2	3

Use deductive logic to complete the grid so that each row, each column, and each 3 by 3 box contains the numbers 1 through 9 in some order. The solution is unique.

A-mazing Twists

Start your way at the top left of this maze and exit on the bottom right. There are so many twists and turns you might think you're in aerobics class.

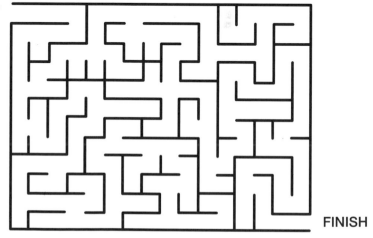

START

FINISH

Answers on page 175.

Word Columns

Find the hidden quote by using the letters directly below each of the blank squares.
Each letter is used only once.

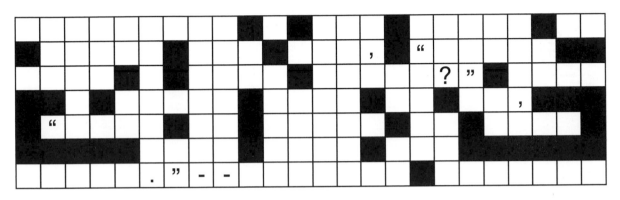

```
                                    i   s
      m       I    a   n     t      a   r
      v h i t    i o    I a s k      g W     e   e
      n a h h s    g e    e a l i e n o o h e a e e
  h a g g t m o c s C g o w n o t t S c h T h e n
  n i i e v o i e e d s h y l e o n w a k r k a z
  S o T e t i m r s n h a r n g s a e m t u l t t
```

Trivia on the Brain

Most people know that the brain is divided into two halves or sides. But did you know that the left side of your brain controls the right side of your body, and the right side of your brain controls the left side of your body?

Answers on page 175.

Go Figure

							42
	4	5		7	3	3	32
7	8	5	2	4			40
8	2			6	5	4	33
6			6	7	3	4	32
4	8		7	5	6		48
	2	5	6			1	28
		5	3		8	3	33
44	29	39	26	41	37	30	42

Fill each square in the grid with a digit from 1 through 9. When the numbers in each row are added, you should arrive at the total in the right-hand column. When the numbers in each column are added, you should arrive at the total on the bottom line. The numbers in each corner-to-corner diagonal must add up to the totals in the upper- and lower-right corners.

Word Ladder

Change just one letter on each line to go from the top word to the bottom word. Do not change the order of the letters. You must have a common English word at each step.

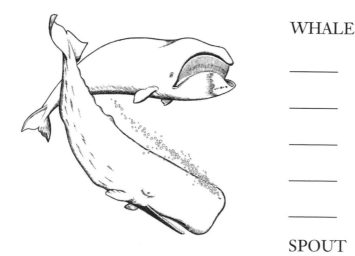

WHALE

_____

_____

_____

_____

_____

SPOUT

Answers on page 175.

Secret Cities?

Cryptograms are messages in substitution code. Break the code to read the message. For example, THE SMART CAT might become FVO QWGDF JGF if **F** is substituted for **T**, **V** for **H**, **O** for **E**, and so on. The code is the same for each cryptogram below.

HINT: Look for repeated letters. **E, T, A, O, N, R,** and **I** are the most-often used letters. The following cryptograms are cities (and their states' postal abbreviations) that start with the letter B.

1. L C H J E B A D I, B G

2. L C O A F F I, F M

3. L A P H E F K K D I I F, A N

4. L A R J A F, B C

5. L C F K A D, B I

6. L Q J J I, B J

7. L A E R I, E G

8. L E R B C D S Z, F G

9. L D C F R A F, B A

10. L E H H E F K R, B J

11. L E D B E F K N C B, C H

Wacky Wordy

Can you "read" the phrase below?

KNEE
SIGN

Answers on page 175.

Star Power

ATTENTION   LOGIC   PLANNING

Fill in each of the empty squares in the grid so that each star is surrounded by the numbers 1 through 8 with no repeats.

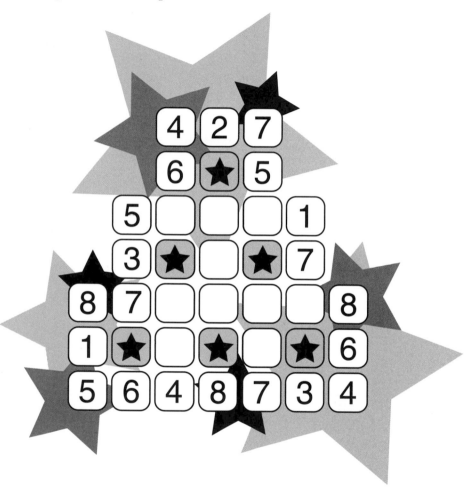

Trivia on the Brain

Did you know that an ostrich's eye is bigger than its brain?

Answers on page 175.

Acrostic Clues

Solve the clues below and then place the letters in their corresponding spots in the grid to reveal a historic quote. The letter in the upper-right corner of each grid square refers to the clue the letter comes from.

1 B	2 K	3 B	4 H	5 E		6 A	7 E	8 C		9 H	10 F	11 G	12 E	13 J	14 C		15 A	16 H
17 C	18 I	19 D		20 E	21 I	22 G	23 I	24 G		25 E	26 E		27 E	28 B	29 B	30 A	31 E	32 J
33 D	34 G	35 A	36 K		37 K	38 H	39 A		40 C	41 A	42 B	43 F	44 J	45 H			
46 H	47 F	48 B	49 E	50 H	51 C		52 G	53 E		54 F	55 A	56 D	57 A				
58 F	59 G	60 I	61 H	62 J	63 D		64 K	65 A		66 A	67 A	68 B		69 K	70 G	71 F	72 A
73 G	74 D		75 H	76 D	77 J	78 A	79 J										

A. Author of quote (2 words)

— — — — — — — — — — — —
(72) (35) (55) (41) (66)(57)(78)(30) (6) (65)(39)(67)(15)

B. Eighth planet from the sun

— — — — — — —
(42) (3) (48) (1) (28)(29)(68)

C. Largest Greek island

— — — — —
(40) (51) (8) (17) (14)

D. Restrain with shackles

— — — — — —
(74) (56) (63) (33) (19)(76)

E. Automotive unit of measure

— — — — — — — — — —
(27) (53) (31) (25) (5) (12)(26)(20)(49) (7)

F. Feel contrite

— — — — — —
(71) (10) (47) (58) (43)(54)

G. Eastern _____ Church

— — — — — — — —
(73) (22) (52) (34) (11)(24)(70)(59)

H. French emperor

— — — — — — — — —
(75) (38) (16) (50) (9) (46) (4) (45)(61)

I. Ness or Lomond

— — — —
(23) (21) (60) (18)

J. Distribute strategically

— — — — — —
(79) (77) (62) (13) (44)(32)

K. _____ or flight

— — — — —
(69) (64) (37) (2) (36)

Answers on page 175.

A Puzzling Perspective

Mentally arrange the lettered balls from large to small in the correct order to spell an 11-letter word.

Clue: Big bad wolf

Sudoku

LOGIC

Use deductive logic to complete the grid so that each row, each column, and each 3 by 3 box contains the numbers 1 through 9 in some order. The solution is unique.

		9		3	5	7		6
			4				9	
2				7				4
1	3					4	6	
		6		4		3		
	7	4					2	1
3				9				8
	2				8			
8		7	3	2		6		

Answers on page 176.

Colorful Scramblegram

Four 6-letter words, all of which revolve around the same theme, have been jumbled. Unscramble the 4 words and write the answers in the space next to each one. Next, transfer the letters that are in the shaded boxes into the empty spaces below and unscramble the 8-letter word that goes with the theme. The theme for this puzzle is color shades.

R E I C E S

L I V E R S

M A D K A S

I N S A N E

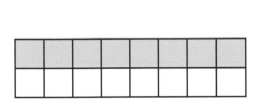

Word Ladder

Change just one letter on each line to go from the top word to the bottom word. Do not change the order of the letters. You must have a common English word at each step.

PEAR

_____

_____

_____

_____

PLUM

Answers on page 176.

Horsing Around

ACROSS

1. Cambodian's neighbor
5. Communist island
9. Lotus programs co.
12. _____ sod
13. Mimicked
14. Miss Piggy's pronoun
15. Taken the place of
17. It has a small head
18. Forget a horse?
20. Radiation protection no.
21. Some batters (abbr.)
22. Trumpet location
25. In a state of joy
30. Way to a dark horse?
33. Not type A
34. Former White House resident's inits.
35. Bumbling bloke
36. PD notice
39. Lighter version of the iron horse?

45. To write quickly
46. Gingham dog fighter
48. Hail
49. Coast-to-coast highway
50. Not a one
51. Color of Santa's suit
52. Fashion designer Cassini
53. They, in Italian

DOWN

1. Keep the rhythm, perhaps
2. Chuck
3. Ship's safe side
4. Innovation beginnings
5. 1962 movie thriller remade in 1991
6. Doing
7. "Where have you _____?"
8. Increased
9. Identity thief
10. One way to cook cabbage
11. Tea flavorer
16. Winner of the Hart Trophy in the NHL
19. Arctic fish
22. List-ending abbr.
23. Melodramatic cry
24. Sent in another direction
26. B followers
27. Pretty mad

28. Descartes' conclusion
29. Nancy Grace's employer
31. Paper quantity
32. Ex _____ (by virtue of position)
37. Army rank (abbr.)
38. Hard stuff
39. Between open and closed
40. Nothing, in a set
41. Abbr. in many U.S. org. names
42. 1997 Peter Fonda title role
43. Key cards in 21
44. "_____ and the Real Girl" (2007 movie)
47. Head opposite

Answers on page 176.

Red, White, and Blue

Each row, column, and corner-to-corner diagonal contains 2 red squares, 2 white squares, and 2 blue squares. Can you complete the grid with the clues below?

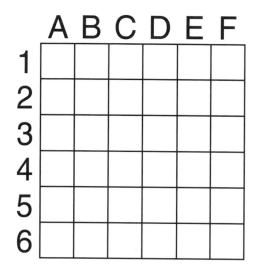

ROW HINTS

1. There are no blues in cells D, E, and F.
2. The pattern of colors takes the form abcabc.
4. Both the blues are somewhere between both the reds.
6. The blues are separated by three cells.

COLUMN HINTS

A. Each red is directly above each white.
B. Both the reds are somewhere between both the whites.
C. The pattern of colors takes the form abcabc.
D. The blues are adjacent.
F. The pattern of colors takes the form abccba.

Word Jigsaw

Fit the pieces into the frame to form common, uncapitalized words reading across and down crossword-style. There's no need to rotate the pieces; they'll fit as shown, with each piece used exactly once.

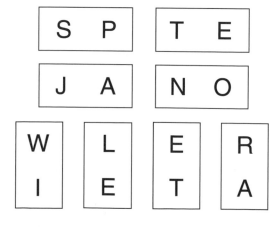

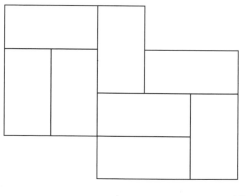

Answers on page 176.

What's Wrong With This Picture?

A street fair can be really fun, but there are 15 things wrong here that can ruin the good time (or at least take attention away from all the shops and activities). Can you identify all the problems and help clean up this street?

Answers on page 176.

Number Crossword

Fill in this crossword with numbers instead of letters. Use the clues to determine which number from 1 through 9 belongs in each empty square. No zeros are used.

ACROSS

1. A multiple of 11
3. A square number
5. Consecutive digits, descending
7. A square number
8. Consecutive odd digits, in some order
10. Digits add up to 4
11. A prime number

DOWN

1. A multiple of 3
2. A palindrome whose digits add up to 18
3. Consecutive odd digits, ascending
4. An even number
6. Consecutive digits, out of order
8. A multiple of 7
9. An odd number

Find the Word

Ignoring spaces, capitalization, and punctuation, find all 16 occurrences of the consecutive letters B-E-A-R in the paragraph below.

Abe arranged to meet his main babe, Ariel, at the fab earring emporium in the mall. Abe applied for a job earlier so he could be a real provider for Ariel when they wed. Ariel, a wannabe artist and a bit overbearing, told Abe a ring wasn't enough and that she wanted matching hoop earrings, a robe, a redwood house like her forebears, and a lamb. Earnest but realistic, Abe scratched his beard, decided he didn't like having to rub earlobes, and quit his job. Ariel couldn't bear the embarrassment that the job didn't earn Abe a red cent and left him just as another babe, a redhead, caught his eye.

Answers on pages 176–177.

Make a Beeline ATTENTION   LANGUAGE   VISUAL SEARCH

This word search is a hive of activity because 27 words, phrases, and names that start with the letter "B" are hidden in the grid below. The words can be found in a straight line horizontally, vertically, or diagonally and may read backward or forward.

```
K S O R K A Y A M J Q L B T D T B
Y L L E B R E E B A G L U E Z S A
J M L R E N R U B K C A B K B E T
T R A I S P C T H X T B B N E U H
R F D E B Y E A A I F D L A L L I
A X B E B O O O S N Q R E L T B N
E O E E B E L B M U B A B B B Y G
B B A G S J C A D L N I A H U B B
K T U V A P P N F A B L T C C A E
C O B L X B F A A F B L H A K B A
A L R D M H N N W L U I Q E L A U
L L I B E L C A N R A B D B E N T
B A D S E N O B E R A B U Z A K Y
D B G G N A B G I B E X V S Z B V
E H E W T A B L L A B E S A B O R
U R S Z G S I I N I S A B T A O B
B A R B E L L S B L U E B O O K Y
```

BABY BLUES	BANK BOOK	BEAN BAG	BLUE BOOK
BACK BURNER	BARBELLS	BEAU BRIDGES	BOAT BASIN
BAD BOYS	BARE BONES	BEER BELLY	BUBBLE BATH
BAKED BEANS	BARNACLE BILL	BELT BUCKLE	BUFFALO BILL
BALANCE BEAM	BASEBALL BAT	BIG BANG	BUMBLEBEE
BALLOT BOX	BATHING BEAUTY	BILLIARD BALL	BUSBOY
BANANA BOAT	BEACH BLANKET	BLACK BEAR	

Answers on page 177.

Fitting Words

In this miniature crossword, the clues are listed randomly and are numbered for convenience only. It is up to you to figure out the placement of the 9 answers. To help you out, we've inserted one letter in the grid, and this is the only occurrence of that letter in the puzzle.

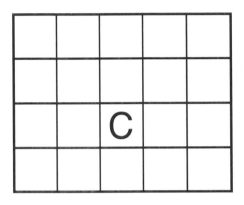

CLUES

1. Youngsters
2. Elm or maple
3. In the know
4. Addlebrained
5. Gem surface
6. Pool table triangle
7. Pub game
8. Complete collections
9. On vacation

See Your Way Free

You seem to have somehow wandered into a kaleidoscope. Now you need to find your way out before someone shakes it and you get all pixilated.

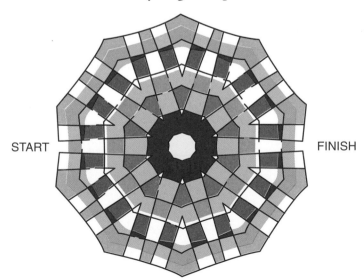

START   FINISH

Answers on page 177.

Hinky Pinky

The clues below lead to a 2-word answer that rhymes, such as Big Pig or Stable Table. The numbers in parentheses after the clue give the number of syllables in each word.

1. Intense anger of a trial panel (2): _____

2. One who deliberately avoids a marathon competitor (2): _____

3. Zealous butler or maid (2): _____

4. Most self-satisfied pharmacist (2): _____

5. Promoting the benefits of youth activities in dens or troops (2): _____

Four-Thought Required

Fill in the blanks in the sentences below with 4-letter words that are anagrams (rearrangements of the same letters) of one another.

1. The _____ ingredient put into the soup was the _____.

2. The couple made up after the angry _____ they had in the _____ week.

3. The car loan _____ when I _____ the final payment.

4. Calla was in a bad _____ after watching the movie "Days of _____."

5. Steven was assigned to _____ the poorly written _____ book.

6. The man _____ the day that he had been _____ to his friend.

7. Because we're so late, we'll probably be at the _____ of the theater, since it's _____ to find middle-row seats this close to showtime.

8. I really _____ the summer _____, so I choose to stay indoors.

9. We _____ told to fill the large _____ with water.

Answers on page 177.

NOW YOUR NOODLE IS COOKING

Sudoku

LOGIC

Use deductive logic to complete the grid so that each row, each column, and each 3 by 3 box contains the numbers 1 through 9 in some order. The solution is unique.

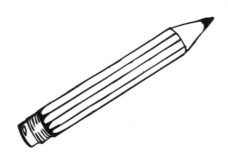

5			7				8	3
			2	9				
3	4				8			
6				8		4		
			9		7			
		3		2				8
			5				2	1
				3	2			
9	7				4			5

Fashionable Anagrams

LANGUAGE

Fill in the blanks in the sentence below with 8-letter words that are anagrams (rearrangements of the same letters) of one another.

The clothing _____ was _____ to the fact that his work wasn't good enough, so he decided to _____ the entire fall collection.

Answers on page 177.

70

Traffic Tango

The 4 pedestrians at the bottom of the maze each need to get where they're going. Destination 1 is a store, 2 is a car, 3 is a home, and 4 is a bicycle. Use the visual clues to decide who is going where, and then guide each on his or her way. Their paths will cross, so don't let them end up in the wrong place!

Answers on page 178.

Pork Puzzler

At the county fair hog competition, best friends Gomer, Homer, Romer, and Domer entered the 4 different breeds of hogs they had raised during the past year. While the friends ate deep-fried Twinkies and awaited the results, the judge hung the ribbons in each hog pen. Unfortunately, the smell of the Twinkies made the hogs hungry and they ate the ribbons. When the friends returned, the judge told them what he remembered. Homer's Hampshire did not finish last. Romer's hog came in third. The Berkshire hog came in first. Gomer's hog finished ahead of the Chester White, and the Duroc finished ahead of Domer's hog. Which hog was raised by which friend, and in which order did they finish?

Word Circle

Complete each 6-letter word so the last 2 letters of the first word are the first 2 letters of the second word, and the last 2 letters of the second word are the first 2 letters of the third word, etc. The last 2 letters of the final word are the first 2 letters of the first word, thus completing the circle.

$$\_\ \_\ L\ L\ \_\ R$$

$$\_\ \_\ O\ U\ \_\ \_$$

$$\_\ \_\ Q\ U\ \_\ \_$$

$$\_\ \_\ E\ V\ E\ \_$$

$$\_\ \_\ T\ I\ \_\ \_$$

Answers on page 178.

Go Figure

Fill each square in the grid with a digit from 1 through 6. When the numbers in each row are multiplied, you should arrive at the total in the right-hand column. When the numbers in each column are multiplied, you should arrive at the total on the bottom line. The numbers in each corner-to-corner diagonal must multiply to the totals in the upper- and lower-right corners.

768

2				6	720
	5		4		120
	3	4		1	120
3		4	3		144
	5			3	120

48 450 384 300 72   360

Hinky Pinky

The clues below lead to a 2-word answer that rhymes, such as Big Pig or Stable Table. The numbers in parentheses after the clue give the number of syllables in each word.

1. Most superior bird's home (1): _____

2. Give sustenance to a warhorse (1): _____

3. Forests owned by Robin of Sherwood Forest (1): _____

4. Stage performer's farm vehicles (2): _____

5. Actively against asking the big question (3): _____

Answers on page 178.

Fruit Salad

ACROSS

1. Rivers of comedy
5. Collect
10. Tabloid mention
14. Exile isle
15. Programming language
16. Writer/director Ephron
17. Larynx part
19. Publicist's concern
20. Certain Asian American
21. "My boy…"
22. Word in old matrimonial rites
23. Lady dealing in futures?
26. 1965 march site
28. Pry
30. Browning work
33. Mule of song
36. Exodus figure
38. Baby grand, perhaps?
39. Old TV's "_____ Three Lives"
41. Kind of code

43. Quotation notation
44. Half of 1960s quartet
46. Reporter's coup
48. Bass, for one
49. Cue
51. Inbox contents
53. _____ Ark
55. Deadlock
59. Soapstone component
61. "Boola-Boola" singer
63. Ties up
64. Airline since 1948
65. Midday appointments, maybe
68. Actor Rob of "Masquerade"
69. Gates licensed it to IBM in 1981
70. Vaquero's weapon
71. Not as much
72. Gives _____ (cares)
73. Sole

DOWN

1. Denims
2. Nostalgic number
3. Humiliate
4. Stoolies, sometimes
5. Lawyers' org.
6. It'll give you a sense of direction
7. They're filled with venom
8. Missile shelters
9. Play parts
10. Sleepless state
11. Project head
12. Pennsylvania port
13. Lots of
18. Saint Catherine's hometown
24. Ivory bar?
25. Wounds
27. An arborist might do it
29. _____ de Leon
31. Organic compound
32. Pitch
33. Fool
34. Winged
35. Vehicle buyers' protection
37. "Whither thou goest" addressee
40. Ancient Greek associated with a sword
42. Good earth
45. Upscale bath feature
47. Spoke (up)
50. Louise's film friend
52. Certain washbowl
54. Sloppy snow
56. Saint Elizabeth Ann _____
57. Fishhook line
58. English class assignment
59. Relate
60. African succulent
62. _____-European
66. Emulate a pigeon
67. Marshall Plan implementer's monogram

Answers on page 178.

Capital Scramblegram

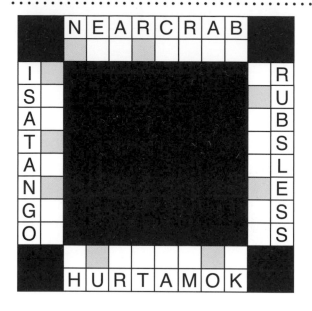

Four 8-letter words, all of which revolve around the same theme, have been jumbled. Unscramble the 4 words and write the answers in the space next to each one. Next, transfer the letters that are in the shaded boxes into the empty spaces below and unscramble the 9-letter word that goes with the theme. The theme for this puzzle is world capitals.

Numbers Game

COMPUTATION

Which 4-figure number that consists of 4 different digits meets the following criteria?

1. The first digit is twice the value of the fourth digit and 2 more than the second digit.

2. The third digit is 1 more than the first digit and 5 more than the fourth digit.

Trivia on the Brain
Did you know that the colors you see are actually registered in your brain, not in your eyes?

Answers on page 178.

Star Power

Fill in each of the empty squares in the grid so that each star is surrounded by the numbers 1 through 8 with no repeats.

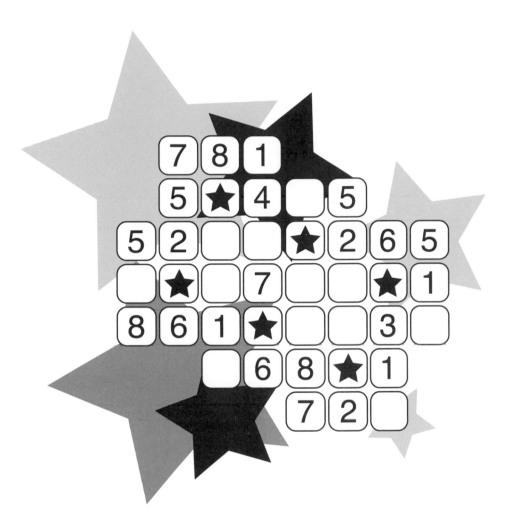

Answers on page 178.

Find the Word

ATTENTION   LANGUAGE   VISUAL SEARCH

Ignoring spaces, capitalization, and punctuation, find all 15 occurrences of the consecutive letters R-O-O-F in the paragraph below.

Rufus was a kangaroo fanatic, and the proof was the kangaroo frescoes he painted on his roof. Rufus owned a bistro, often bringing home food for his pet kangaroo, Fido. Fido, a box-ing kangaroo, was a semipro, often fighting large wallabies. His win total was zero, officially, although he once defeated a koala in an unofficial match when the smaller koala pulled a switcheroo, falling to throw the fight. Rufus kept Fido in a leakproof hut with shatterproof windows and read him stories of the jackaroo, fantastic creatures that were part rabbit and

part kangaroo. Fido didn't believe the stories but played along because he had no proof and wanted Rufus to keep bringing foods from the bistro, of which the rooster fondue was his favorite.

Word Jigsaw

LANGUAGE   SPATIAL PLANNING

Fit the pieces into the frame to form common, uncapitalized words reading across and down crossword-style. There's no need to rotate the pieces; they'll fit as shown, with each piece used exactly once.

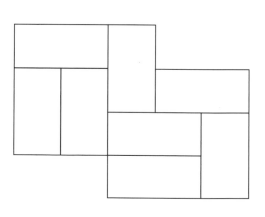

Answers on page 179.

Remember Me? (Part 1)

Look at the group of pictures for 2 minutes and remember their names. Then turn the page, and see how many of the 9 objects you remember.

Soccer Ball   Duck   Flowers

Nurse   Lawnmower   Hammer

Spoon   Lobster   Seahorse

Remember Me? (Part 2)

(Do not read this until you have read the previous page!)

Put a checkmark next to the words you saw on the preceding page:

____ Trumpet	____ Duck	____ Nurse
____ Obelisk	____ Cloud	____ Violin
____ Seahorse	____ Lobster	____ Lawnmower
____ Dollar	____ Spoon	____ Teapot
____ Soccer Ball	____ Camera	____ Hammer
	____ Flowers	

More Times the Fun

Enter the digits 1 through 6 into the grid so each row and each column contains each digit only once. The number inside each circle is the product of the 4 digits that surround it.

The grid contains:
- Row 1: 4 (second column), 60 (circle), 5, 48 (circle), 15 (circle)
- 6, 144 (circle), 225 (circle), 5
- 1, 4, 240 (circle)
- 30 (circle)
- 3
- 5, 6

Answers on page 179.

Candy's Collectibles

Candy's cabinet is filled with similar knickknacks, but only 2 of them are exact matches. Can you find them?

Answer on page 179.

Fitting Words

In this miniature crossword, the clues are listed randomly and are numbered for convenience only. It is up to you to figure out the placement of the 9 answers. To help you out, we've inserted one letter in the grid, and this is the only occurrence of that letter in the puzzle.

CLUES

1. Awaken
2. Sky-hued
3. Mollify
4. Track events
5. The "windows to the soul"
6. Aesop creation
7. Skin cream ingredient
8. Endure
9. Old MacDonald's place

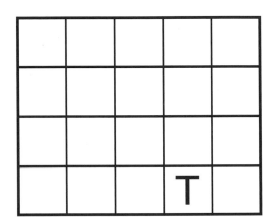

Number Square

Each lettered box in the grid contains a number from 1 through 9. Use the clues to put the digits in their proper places. Each number is used only once.

A	B	C
D	E	F
G	H	J

CLUES

1. The top row contains only multiples of 3
2. The far-right column contains only even digits
3. E + F = A + G
4. B + H = J

Answers on page 179.

Letterbox Aviary

The letters in WREN can be found in boxes 13, 19, 23, and 26, but not necessarily in that order. Similarly, the letters in all the other birds' names can be found in the boxes indicated. Insert all the letters of the alphabet into the boxes; if you do this correctly, the shaded cells will reveal the names of two more birds.

Hint: Look for words that share a single letter. For example, DUCK shares a U with QUAIL and a C with FALCON. By comparing the number lists, you can then deduce the values of these letters.

1	2	3	4	5	6	7	8	9	10	11	12	13

14	15	16	17	18	19	20	21	22	23	24	25	26

BUZZARD: 4, 8, 11, 17, 19, 21

DUCK: 1, 8, 9, 11

FALCON: 4, 9, 18, 20, 23, 24

HOBBY: 5, 12, 20, 21

JACKDAW: 1, 3, 4, 9, 11, 13

KITE: 1, 2, 22, 26

MAGPIE: 4, 6, 7, 16, 22, 26

OSPREY: 5, 7, 14, 19, 20, 26

PHOENIX: 7, 12, 15, 20, 22, 23, 26

QUAIL: 4, 8, 10, 22, 24

RAVEN: 4, 19, 23, 25 26

WREN: 13, 19, 23, 26

Answers on page 179.

A Puzzling Perspective

Mentally arrange the lettered balls from large to small in the correct order to spell an 11-letter word.

Clue: Myopic

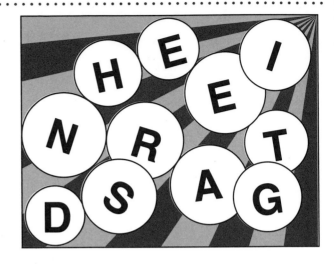

Code-Doku

LOGIC

		O						V
	E		I	F				O
	F				A			
E	A		N	I				F
			E		V			
V								E
		E			L	N		
	L		N		E			
	F	I	V		L			

Use deductive logic to complete the grid so that each row, each column, and each 3 by 3 box contains the letters in the words FINAL VOTE. When you have completed the puzzle, read the shaded squares to find something you might sip.

Answers on page 180.

Start Your Day by Alpha Sleuth™

Move each of the letters below into the grid to form common words. You will use each letter only once. The letters in the numbered cells of the grid correspond to the letters in the phrase below the grid. Completing the grid will help you complete the phrase, and vice versa. When finished, the grid and phrase should be filled with valid words, and you will have used all the letters in the letter set. The letters already included in the grid will help get you started.

HINT: The numbered cells in the grid are arranged alphabetically, so the letter in the cell marked 1 will appear in the alphabet before the letter in the cell marked 2, and so on.

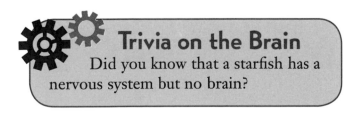

A B C D E F G H I J K L M N O P Q R S T U V W X Y Z

Trivia on the Brain
Did you know that a starfish has a nervous system but no brain?

Answers on page 180.

Sudoku

			7					6
	1	4		6		2		
6			5					8
	2		9					
	6		8		2		4	
				5		6		
7				3				2
	9		1			5	3	
3				2				

Use deductive logic to complete the grid so that each row, each column, and each 3 by 3 box contains the numbers 1 through 9 in some order. The solution is unique.

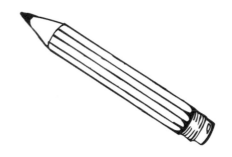

Desert Island Quiz

While fishing for perch, Dean and Jerry accidentally hooked a killer whale that dragged their little boat to a deserted uncharted island where the boat crashed, stranding the unlucky fishermen. Having only a pencil and a puzzle book to pass the time, Dean and Jerry quickly solved every puzzle in the book and became bored. Jerry decided it was time to come up with his own puzzle. He handed Dean the puzzle book and asked him to secretly tear out a page. Jerry then told Dean to add up the remaining page numbers and tell him the total. When Dean said, "The total is 90," Jerry immediately knew the page numbers on the page Dean tore out and how many pages were originally in the book. What were the answers?

Answers on page 180.

Letterbox Zoo

The letters in IBEX can be found in boxes 4, 8, 10, and 20, but not necessarily in that order. Similarly, the letters in all the other animals' names can be found in the boxes indicated. Insert all the letters of the alphabet into the boxes; if you do this correctly, the shaded cells will reveal the names of 2 more critters.

Hint: Look for words that share a single letter. For example, IBEX shares a B with BUFFALO and an E with MOOSE. By comparing the number lists, you can then deduce the values of these letters.

1	2	3	4	5	6	7	8	9	10	11	12	13

14	15	16	17	18	19	20	21	22	23	24	25	26

AARDVARK: 5, 6, 9, 11, 17

BUFFALO: 4, 5, 14, 18, 19, 26

CHEETAH: 1, 5, 8, 23, 25

DONKEY: 6, 8, 11, 16, 19, 21

GIRAFFE: 5, 7, 8, 9, 10, 18

HORSE: 1, 2, 8, 9, 19

IBEX: 4, 8, 10, 20

JAGUAR: 5, 7, 9, 14, 24

MOOSE: 2, 8, 15, 19

SPRINGBOK: 2, 4, 7, 9, 10, 11, 12, 19, 21

SQUIRREL: 2, 8, 9, 10, 14, 22, 26

TIGER: 7, 8, 9, 10, 25

WEASEL: 2, 3, 5, 8, 26

ZEBRA: 4, 5, 8, 9, 13

Answers on page 180.

Now Your Noodle Is Cooking

What's Wrong With This Picture?

This game of hoops is filled with hijinks—20, in fact. We know it's a tall order, but can you find them all before the fans cry foul?

Answers on page 180.

Number Crossword

Fill in this crossword with numbers instead of letters. Use the clues to determine which number from 1 through 9 belongs in each empty square. No zeros are used.

ACROSS

1. A power of 2
4. Consecutive digits, descending
5. The sum of its digits is 15
6. An even number
7. Its digits are in descending order
9. A square number

DOWN

1. Two different digits
2. A palindrome
3. A power of 2
4. Four identical digits
5. Its middle digit is the sum of its 2 outside digits
8. A square number

Widget Bewilderment

COMPUTATION

Dick has one-and-a-third as many widgets as Tom, and Harry has one-and-a-third as many as Dick. Together, they have 74 widgets. How many widgets does each man have?

Trivia on the Brain

Research has shown that the newest cells in your brain learn more quickly than the more "mature" brain cells.

Answers on page 180.

Merry Christmas

ACROSS

1. _____ 'n' roll music
5. _____-ovo vegetarian
10. Frosts a cake
14. Press, as a laundered shirt
15. Take _____ for the worse
16. Loathsome
17. Genealogical chart: 2 wds.
19. New Haven school
20. Makes very happy
21. _____-Tzu (Taoism founder)
22. Bank offering
23. Swedish car
25. Adjust, as a piano
27. Alphabetical introduction
30. Q-Tip, e.g.
32. Copied, in a way
36. Auto warmer: 2 wds.
39. Ancient Greek marketplace

40. Award for best ad
41. Affirmatives
43. _____ Bator (Mongolia's capital)
44. Lively dances
46. Miniature sculpture
48. Confuses
50. "Shoo!"
51. "Mayday!"
52. Feminine org. since 1855
54. End of the work wk. cry
56. Ship's personnel
59. World Series mo.
61. Parisian places of learning
65. Model anew
66. Film director's cry after a successful take: 3 wds.
68. The "A" in A.D.
69. Hip joints: ECO AX anagram
70. Misplace
71. Sweat unit
72. Raise with a crane
73. Snick and _____

DOWN

1. Widespread
2. By mouth
3. Extremely deep sleep
4. Makes booties, maybe
5. Uses a certain store payment plan: 2 wds.
6. Court figure: Abbr.
7. Hair ringlet
8. "Trick or _____!"
9. Early inning status: 2 wds.
10. Association including Harvard and Princeton: 2 wds.
11. "Ta-ta, Antonio!"
12. Jazzy Fitzgerald
13. Spotted
18. Renter's document
24. Motel in "Psycho"
26. Second Amendment rights grp.
27. Ghana's capital
28. Bundled, as hay
29. Wept
31. Outdoes
33. Young male horses
34. Poet's muse
35. Copenhagen natives
37. Los Angeles movie center
38. Giggle when tickled, say
42. Broadway assembly: 2 wds.
45. Use a Singer
47. Central New York city on the Mohawk
49. Type of whiskey
53. Sneeze sound
55. Chickens and ducks, e.g.
56. Seafood choice
57. Philosopher Descartes
58. _____ St. Vincent Millay
60. Cab
62. Scientology's _____ Hubbard
63. Leisure
64. World War I German admiral
67. Prof's helpers, briefly

Answers on page 181.

Red, White, and Blue

Each row, column, and corner-to-corner diagonal contains 2 red squares, 2 white squares, and 2 blue squares. Can you complete the grid with the clues below?

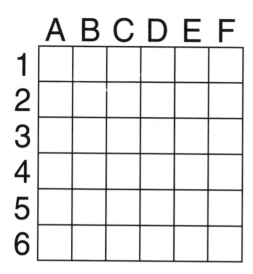

ROW HINTS

1. The whites are adjacent.
2. The pattern of colors takes the form abcabc.
3. The whites and the reds are between the blues.
4. The whites are somewhere between the blues.
5. The pattern of colors takes the form abccba.
6. The blues are somewhere between the whites.

COLUMN HINTS

A. Each red is directly above each white.
C. Each red is directly above each white.
F. The reds are somewhere between the whites.

Wacky Wordy

Can you "read" the word below?

STEFRANKIN

Trivia on the Brain

Your brain accounts for only about 2 percent of your body weight, but it uses more than 20 percent of your body's oxygen supply.

Answers on page 181.

Read Between the Lines

Which figure comes next?

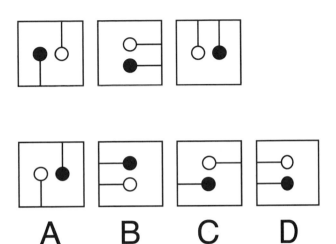

Name Calling

Decipher the encoded word in the quip below using the numbers and letters on the phone pad. Remember that each number can stand for 3 or 4 possible letters.

It turns out Pikes isn't the pinnacle because 2–6–5–6–7–2–3–6 has 26 that are higher.

Answers on page 181.

Acrostic Clues

Solve the clues below and then place the letters in their corresponding spots in the grid to reveal a quote about the brain. The letter in the upper-right corner of each grid square refers to the clue the letter comes from.

1 B	2 E		3 C	4 I	5 D	6 A	7 J		8 A	9 H	10 A	11 C	12 G	13 B	14 B	
15 E	16 H	17 A	18 F	19 C	20 A	21 B		22 I	23 B	24 I	25 A	26 H		27 D	28 A	
29 H	30 D	31 I	32 B	33 B		34 J	35 I	36 I	37 D		38 H	39 G	40 C	41 A	42 E	43 J	44 G
45 G	46 D	47 D	48 H	49 A	50 E	51 F		52 J	53 A	54 G	55 I		56 J	57 H	58 F	59 A	60 J	61 J	62 B
63 A	64 E	65 J	66 I	67 I	68 F	69 H	70 C	71 F		72 A	73 A	74 B		75 G	76 G	77 E	78 G
79 A	80 E	81 I	82 I	83 J	84 F	

A. Renaissance artist, inventor, and author of quote (3 words)

— — — — — — — — — — — — — — — — —
(25) (49) (28) (17) (72) (6)   (8) (20) (59) (53) (10) (79) (73) (63) (41)

B. Absent-minded fantasies

— — — — — — — — —
(14) (1) (33) (74) (32) (13) (23) (21) (62)

C. Plunged

— — — — —
(70) (11) (40) (3) (19)

D. Fully owned, as in stock options

— — — — — —
(30) (5) (27) (47) (46) (37)

E. Type of computer

— — — — — — —
(42) (50) (2) (15) (80) (64) (77)

Answers on page 181.

94

F. Mushroom, e.g.

— — — — — —
(84) (58) (51) (18) (68)(71)

G. Breaks up

— — — — — — — —
(12) (39) (78) (45) (76)(54)(44)(75)

H. Most breezy

— — — — — — — —
(48) (16) (69) (38) (9) (29)(26)(57)

I. In an obnoxious manner

— — — — — — — — — — —
(67) (66) (22) (82) (36)(81)(35) (4) (31)(24)(55)

J. To a great extent

— — — — — — — — — —
(60) (52) (34) (61) (65)(56)(43)(83) (7)

Code-Doku

	L			A	G	T		
			E					
G		T	L	N		S		
S		O						M
				L		A		
							O	
E	N			O	G	M		
T		G		A	E			

Use deductive logic to complete the grid so that each row, each column, and each 3 by 3 box contains the letters in the words A LONG STEM. When you have completed the puzzle, read the shaded squares to describe something you might see at the beach.

Answers on page 181.

A Puzzling Perspective

Mentally arrange the lettered balls from large to small in the correct order to spell an 11-letter word.

Clue: Approaching

Fitting Words

LANGUAGE · LOGIC · PLANNING

In this miniature crossword, the clues are listed randomly and are numbered for convenience only. It is up to you to figure out the placement of the 9 answers. To help you out, we've inserted one letter in the grid, and this is the only occurrence of that letter in the puzzle.

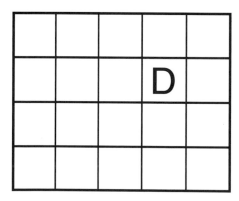

CLUES

1. Walks like an expectant father
2. Stage whisper
3. Not so much
4. Wedding bands
5. Brass component
6. 47-string instrument
7. Eye color
8. Competitive advantage
9. China setting

Answers on page 181.

Law and Disorder

While the sheriff was lost in thought about cattle rustlers and train robberies, a guy in a black hat sneaked into his office and changed a few things. Can you find all 9 changes?

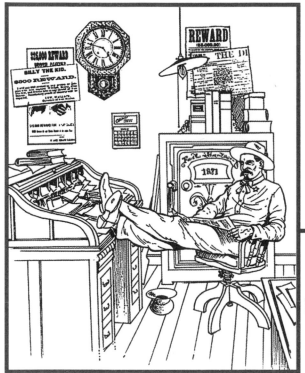

Answers on page 181.

Intergalactic Mix-up

Five aliens have arranged to enter the intergalactic space station in a certain order, but the parking attendant has the details on his

	Name	Race	Planet	Galaxy
1	Azba	Florals	Klink	P37
2	Beggle	Ginnys	Lima	Q21
3	Coot	Hives	Mogda	R11
4	Da	Inklins	Nin	S63
5	Evary	Jollys	Osder	T58

list all mixed up. Although the list above has each item in the correct column, only one item is correctly positioned in each column. The following facts are certain about the correct order:

1. Ginnys, Inklins, and Q21 are not third.
2. Florals is 1 place above Osder.
3. Galaxy S63 is not last.
4. Evary is 2 places above Mogda.
5. Azba is second.
6. Coot is 2 places below galaxy Q21.
7. R11 is 2 places above Inklins.
8. Klink, Osder, and Florals are not fourth.
9. Lima is 2 places below Hives.
10. R11 is 2 places above Da.
11. T58 is fourth.

Can you determine the alien name, race, planet, and galaxy of origin for each position?

Trivia on the Brain

The first known writing about the human brain was found in ancient Sumerian records from around 4000 B.C.

Answers on page 181.

Find the Word

Ignoring spaces, capitalization, and punctuation, locate a noun hidden in each sentence below that can be found in a school.

1. "Oh my, look at that play! Ground ball for sure," Beth's mom said at softball practice.

2. "How could this lock erode inside our spaceship?" Greta asked the captain.

3. "I've always wanted a child. Renting one's not an option, I suppose?" asked the alien regretfully.

4. "At my sleepover, we had a candy orgy! Many of us were sick the next day, too," Michael boasted proudly. "Ugh!" replied Amy.

5. Success! The doctor couldn't wait to tout each errant embryo to the whole scientific community.

6. "It would be an honor to ad loc a fete rialto in Venice for you, my dear," the bearded man told his latest beau in Italian. She swooned prettily and fainted in his arms.

Go Figure

Fill each square in the grid with a digit from 1 through 9. When the numbers in each row are added, you should arrive at the total in the right-hand column. When the numbers in each column are added, you should arrive at the total on the bottom line. The numbers in each corner-to-corner diagonal must add to the totals in the upper- and lower-right corners.

								27
6	2		5	3		5		23
1	3	6		4	5	2		28
6		4	7		8			36
2	1	8		3	5			36
		2	7	5	3	3		33
	4		1			7		28
	5	5		1	4			28
27	33	29	37	22	28	36	37	

Answers on page 182.

Name That Scramblegram

Four 8-letter words, all of which revolve around the same theme, have been jumbled. Unscramble the 4 words and write the answers in the space next to each one. Next, transfer the letters that are in the shaded boxes into the empty spaces below and unscramble the 9-letter word that goes with the theme. The theme for this puzzle is women's names.

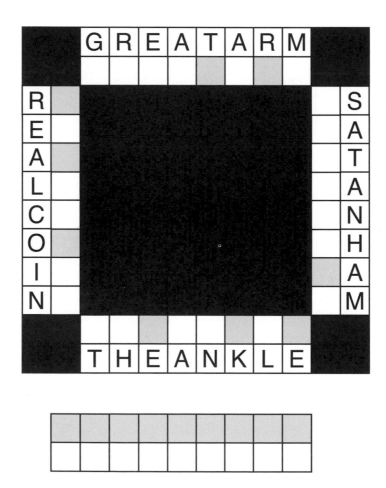

Answers on page 182.

Sudoku

Use deductive logic to complete the grid so that each row, each column, and each 3 by 3 box contains the numbers 1 through 9 in some order. The solution is unique.

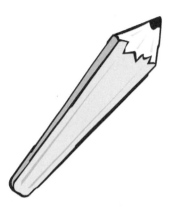

			9				1	
	3						6	
8			1				7	
5				1	3	2		
4			8		7			1
		7	9	2				8
	2				9			3
	4					1		
	9		6					

Word Ladder

Change just one letter on each line to go from the top word to the bottom word. Do not change the order of the letters. You must have a common English word at each step.

BRISK

_____

_____

_____

_____

BLOCK

Answers on page 182.

Colorful Clues

ACROSS

1. What Wednesday's child is full of
4. TV comedian Carey
8. Jupiter has a big red one
12. Shanty
13. Solemn vow
14. Last item in Pandora's box
15. First person in Germany
16. Tubular pasta
17. Cajun thickener
18. Yellow Book listings
21. Quasimodo portrayer Chaney
22. Bear's foot
23. Comic book cry of pain
25. Skater's jump
27. South Korean automaker
30. Little black book listings
33. Pig shelter
34. Elbows in pipe
35. Not so much
36. Metro maker
37. Matador's support
38. Blue book listing

44. Small songbird
45. Female friend in France
46. Poison _____
47. Words of comparison
48. Actor Sean
49. Born
50. Org. with a shuttle program
51. Football positions
52. Word after natural or tear

DOWN

1. Party line enforcer
2. Cry of pain
3. Study of behavior
4. Typical roses order
5. Gutter filler
6. "_____, Brute?"
7. Cries softly
8. She needed taming, according to Shakespeare
9. Start of Ben Franklin's almanac?
10. _____ Dei
11. Cowboy nickname
19. Start of a bedtime prayer: 2 wds.
20. Indonesian island
23. "You are correct, sir!"
24. Phone line abbr.
25. Distribute according to plan
26. Org. that played for one season in 2001

27. Position of prayer
28. Driver's license and the like, abbr.
29. Beast of burden
31. "Walk on the Wild Side" singer Lou
32. Jazz singer Fitzgerald
36. Birthplace of Italian poet Eugenio Montale
37. Kilns
38. Stellar bear
39. Drops below the horizon
40. The last word in churches?
41. Cacao pod covering
42. Layer of the iris
43. They may be peeled
44. Victory

Answers on page 182.

Star Power

Fill in each of the empty squares in the grid so that each star is surrounded by the numbers 1 through 8 with no repeats.

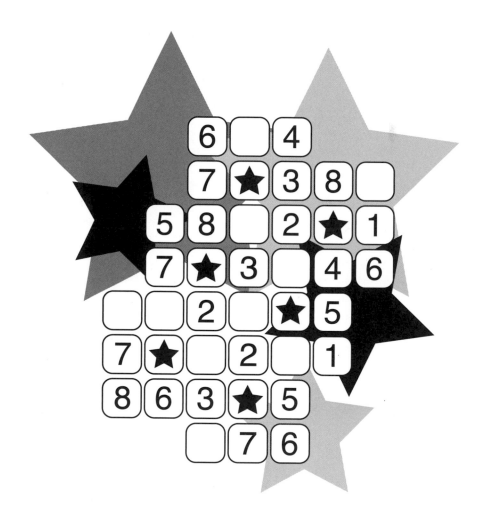

Trivia on the Brain

Your brain can be bruised, just like any other tissue in your body.

Answers on page 182.

A Puzzling Perspective

Mentally arrange the lettered balls from large to small in the correct order to spell an 11-letter word.

Clue: Defaulted debt

Word Jigsaw

Fit the pieces into the frame to form common, uncapitalized words reading across and down crossword-style. There's no need to rotate the pieces; they'll fit as shown, with each piece used exactly once.

Answers on pages 182–183.

Red, White, Blue, and Green

LOGIC

Each row, column, and corner-to-corner diagonal contains 2 red squares, 2 white squares, 2 blue squares, and 2 green squares. Can you complete the grid with the clues below?

ROW HINTS

1. The whites are separated by 5 cells.
2. Each blue is immediately right of each green.
3. The greens cannot be found in cells E, F, G, or H.
4. The greens are adjacent.
5. Two greens and a blue are directly enclosed by the reds.
6. Two blues and a red are directly enclosed by the greens.
7. Two reds and a white are directly enclosed by the blues.
8. The blues are separated by 6 cells.

COLUMN HINTS

A. Three different colors are directly enclosed by the greens.
B. Two whites, 2 blues, and a red are directly enclosed by the greens.
D. Each blue is directly above each white.
E. Each white is directly above each green.
G. Two reds and a white are directly enclosed by the greens.
H. The pattern of colors takes the form abacbcdd.

A B C D E F G H

1
2
3
4
5
6
7
8

Answers on page 183.

Fitting Words

In this miniature crossword, the clues are listed randomly and are numbered for convenience only. It is up to you to figure out the placement of the 9 answers. To help you out, we've inserted one letter in the grid, and this is the only occurrence of that letter in the puzzle.

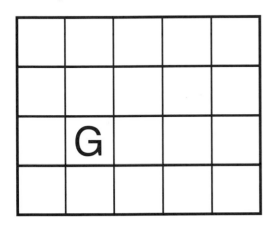

CLUES

1. Butcher's wares
2. Unusual collectible
3. General vicinity
4. Con game
5. 007, for one
6. Pocket debris
7. "_____ We Dance?"
8. Auction units
9. Enormous

Sudoku

Use deductive logic to complete the grid so that each row, each column, and each 3 by 3 box contains the numbers 1 through 9 in some order. The solution is unique.

	2			8		6		
6		4			2			
	9				4			
4				2				
3	1			5			7	9
				3				5
			7				5	
			1			9		8
		6		4			1	

Answers on page 183.

Name Calling

ATTENTION   **VISUAL SEARCH**

Decipher the encoded word in the quip below using the numbers and letters on the phone pad. Remember that each number can stand for 3 or 4 possible letters.

My poor mind works like lightning: one 2–7–4–5–5–4–2–6–8 flash and it is gone!

Word Ladder

LANGUAGE   **PLANNING**

Change just one letter on each line to go from the top word to the bottom word. Do not change the order of the letters. You must have a common English word at each step.

CHIP

———

———

———

———

———

———

DIPS

Answers on page 183.

The Upper Crust
by Alpha Sleuth™

Move each of the letters below into the grid to form common words. You will use each letter only once. The letters in the numbered cells of the grid correspond to the letters in the phrase below the grid. Completing the grid will help you complete the phrase, and vice versa. When finished, the grid and phrase should be filled with valid words, and you will have used all the letters in the letter set. The letters already included in the grid will help get you started.

HINT: The numbered cells in the grid are arranged alphabetically, so the letter in the cell marked 1 will appear in the alphabet before the letter in the cell marked 2, and so on.

A B C D E F G H I J K L M N O P Q R S T U V W X Y Z

| 5 | 4 | 8 | 4 | 6 | 3 |

| 5 | 1 | 7 | 3 | 2 |

Trivia on the Brain

Although most neurons are microscopic—among the smallest cells in the human body—some are large enough to be visible to the naked eye.

Answers on page 183.

Star Power

Fill in each of the empty squares in the grid so that each star is surrounded by the numbers 1 through 8 with no repeats.

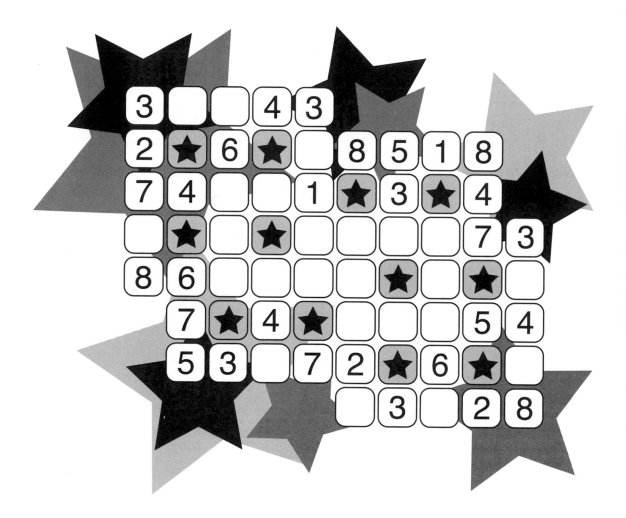

Answers on page 183.

Go Figure

COMPUTATION   LOGIC

Fill each square in the grid with a digit from 1 through 9. When the numbers in each row are added, you should arrive at the total in the right-hand column. When the numbers in each column are added, you should arrive at the total on the bottom line. The numbers in each corner-to-corner diagonal must add to the totals in the upper- and lower-right corners.

44

7				5	2	4	8	42
8		2	8	7		7		55
	7	4	9		7	6	5	49
	6	4			7	6	5	50
5	6	7	2	8			5	51
9	5	4	5	2	8			48
	6		8	7	3	4		47
	4	9		6	5	8	7	42
46	52	39	43	51	47	52	54	56

Tasty Toss

LOGIC

Once a year, the Pie Palace closes its doors to customers and gives its employees a chance to cut loose with a good old-fashioned pie fight. This year, each employee threw his or her favorite flavor of pie (blueberry, strawberry, lemon, and chocolate) and wore an apron that was pie-colored (blue, red, yellow, or brown). However, their aprons were not necessarily the same colors as their favorite pies. In fact, Sam was the only employee whose apron was the same color as the pie he threw. Quinn was not wearing a red or blue apron. Pat threw blueberry pies. The employee in the brown apron threw lemon pies. Rhoda did not throw strawberry pies and did not wear a yellow apron. Which flavor pie did each employee throw, and what color was each person's apron before it was covered with pie?

Answers on page 183.

111

Face the Music

ACROSS

1. Herr von Bismarck
5. Skin doctor's field: abbr.
9. Aptly named fruit
14. "If I may be so bold…"
15. Neighborhood
16. Girl rescued by Don Juan
17. He wrote what was originally called "Defense of Fort M'Henry" in 1814

20. 1968 hit with the lyric "I like the way you walk, I like the way you talk"
21. Prepares text for publication
22. Split pea, e.g.
24. Private address?
25. Econ. yardstick
28. Feed holder
30. Large sea ducks

35. 1964 Oscar-winning actress Kedrova
37. Deep grooves
39. Earth's path
40. "More optimistically..."
43. Sheer curtain fabric
44. Red Cross supplies
45. Slow flow
46. Make beloved
48. Seldom seen
50. "The Spanish Tragedy" dramatist
51. Pro's opposite
53. International org. since 1881
55. Floral ornaments
60. Down Under denizen
64. Seismology tool
66. Kid's song refrain
67. Place in order
68. RAM unit
69. Philosopher Kierkegaard
70. WWW addresses
71. Miss Trueheart, of old comics

DOWN

1. Clumsy sorts
2. Drive-_____ window
3. Afternoon socials
4. Bygone Dodge models
5. Iced rum cocktail
6. Hospital trauma centers: abbr.
7. Nap, maybe
8. "Miracle on 34th Street" store
9. Like some motives
10. Obtains
11. Cotton to
12. "Okay if _____ myself out?"
13. What Simon does, in a kids' game
18. Industry big shots: abbr.
19. Early Ron Howard role
23. Outlet inserts
25. Hand protector
26. Smooth, sheer fabric
27. Kilt's pattern, often
29. Miscellaneous category
31. First 007 movie
32. Online library offering
33. Snazzy
34. Spirited mount
36. Competent
38. Wander off the path
41. Stimulus response
42. Sets aside (for)
47. Campus military org.
49. Old 5-franc pieces
52. Associate of Gandhi
54. Fancy tie
55. AAA travel recommendations
56. The Buckeye State
57. Crystal ball studier
58. New York canal
59. Headliner
61. Rational
62. Spots in the Seine
63. Mouse-sighting shrieks
65. Photo blow-up: abbr.

Answers on page 184.

A Puzzling Perspective

LANGUAGE   SPATIAL VISUALIZATION

Mentally arrange the lettered balls from large to small in the correct order to spell an 11-letter word.

Clue: Upgraded

Word Pyramid

LANGUAGE

Fill in the word pyramid by finding the answer to each clue and writing it on the corresponding step. As you move from the top down, each new word is an anagram of the previous word, with one letter added.

Shanty inspiration

Of sound mind

Trap

Large birds

Deep hollows

Maybe from space?

For juice or wine

Answers on page 184.

Code-Doku

Use deductive logic to complete the grid so that each row, each column, and each 3 by 3 box contains the letters in the words TOXIN SEAL. When you have completed the puzzle, read the shaded squares to form a twist on a well-known adage.

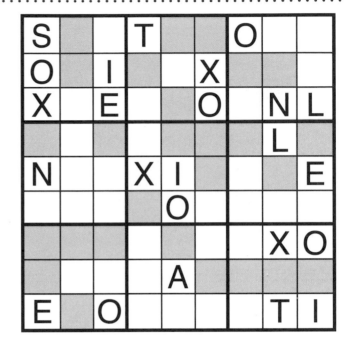

S			T		O			
O		I		X				
X		E		O		N	L	
						L		
N		X	I				E	
			O					
						X	O	
		A						
E	O					T	I	

Animal Anagrams

Fill in the blanks in the sentence below with 7-letter words that are anagrams (rearrangements of the same letters) of one another.

While admiring the small, spotted, leopardlike animals curled up in a refrigerator and sporting designer sunglasses, the zookeeper remarked, "Those are the _____ _____ I've ever seen!"

Answers on page 184.

Acrostic Clues

GENERAL KNOWLEDGE   LANGUAGE

Solve the clues below and then place the letters in their corresponding spots in the grid to reveal an artistic quote. The letter in the upper-right corner of each grid square refers to the clue the letter comes from.

1 H	2 H		3 A	4 G	5 E	6 E	7 H	8 G	9 A		10 I	11 B	12 C					
13 F	14 J	15 E	16 H	17 J	18 A	19 D	20 G	21 F	22 F	23 G	24 G		25 B	26 A		27 A	28 F	29 C
30 A	31 C	32 C	33 J	34 E	35 J		36 B	37 E	38 H		39 D	40 D	41 F	42 F	43 I	44 A		
45 E	46 G	47 B		48 B	49 I	50 C	51 B	52 I	53 D	54 A		55 A	56 E	57 H		58 C	59 C	60 C	61 D
62 G	63 A	64 E		65 J	66 B	67 D		68 A	69 J	70 D		71 E	72 I	73 J				
74 E	75 H	76 D	77 F	78 D	79 F	80 H		81 B	82 I								

A. Author of quote (2 words)

— — — — — — — — — — —
(26) (63) (30) (9) (27) (54) (68) (44) (55) (3) (18)

B. 124th Japanese Emperor

— — — — — — — —
(66) (81) (48) (47) (11) (25) (36) (51)

C. Bivouac

— — — — — — — —
(50) (59) (32) (58) (60) (31) (29) (12)

D. Averted

— — — — — — — — —
(39) (19) (67) (76) (70) (78) (61) (40) (53)

E. Deserving of time or effort

— — — — — — — — — —
(45) (15) (6) (64) (56) (71) (37) (74) (34) (5)

F. Elijah and Ezekiel

— — — — — — — —
(13) (41) (28) (21) (22) (77) (79) (42)

G. Paired with maid or pot

— — — — — — —
(8) (46) (20) (4) (62) (23) (24)

H. Famous physicist

— — — — — — — —
(57) (1) (2) (80) (16) (38) (7) (75)

I. Much warmer

— — — — — —
(72) (43) (82) (10) (49) (52)

J. Cyclone

— — — — — — —
(65) (35) (33) (14) (73) (17) (69)

Answers on page 184.

Word Jigsaw

Fit the pieces into the frame to form common, uncapitalized words reading across and down crossword-style. There's no need to rotate the pieces; they'll fit as shown, with each piece used exactly once.

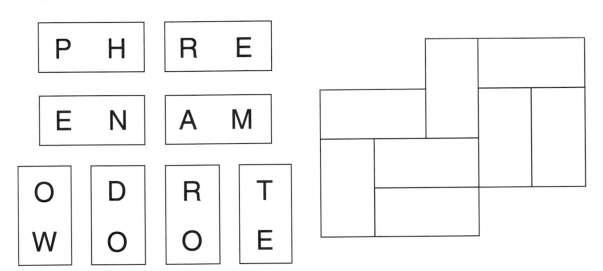

Fill 'Er Up

You need to measure 6 gallons of water, but you only have a 9-gallon bucket (bucket A) and a 4-gallon bucket (bucket B). How do you do this? There is an unlimited water supply, and both buckets start empty.

Answers on page 184.

Sudoku

					1	4		
		6			4		2	
	7			2				5
1	5							9
		3		2				
8							5	2
5				1			9	
	3		8			6		
		7	2					

Use deductive logic to complete the grid so that each row, each column, and each 3 by 3 box contains the numbers 1 through 9 in some order. The solution is unique.

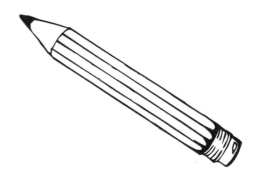

Make Sense of the Symbols

Which figure comes next?

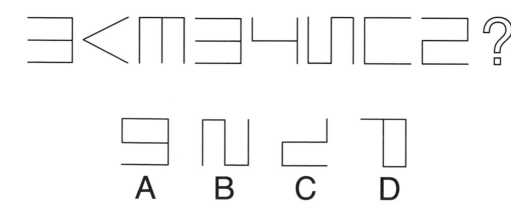

A   B   C   D

Answers on page 184.

Tight Quarters

There isn't much room to maneuver in this maze. Start at the top right, and make your way to the bottom left.

START

FINISH

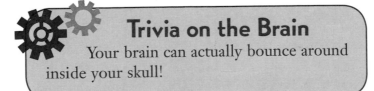

Trivia on the Brain
Your brain can actually bounce around inside your skull!

Answer on page 185.

Stately Letterbox

The letters in UTAH can be found in boxes 4, 5, 15, and 26, but not necessarily in that order. Similarly, the letters in all the other states' names can be found in the boxes indicated. Insert all the letters of the alphabet into the boxes; if you do this correctly, the shaded cells will reveal another state.

Hint: Look for words that share a single letter. For example, OREGON shares an O with WASHINGTON and an R with NEBRASKA. By comparing the number lists, you can then deduce the values of these letters.

1	2	3	4	5	6	7	8	9	10	11	12	13
Q												
14	15	16	17	18	19	20	21	22	23	24	25	26

ARIZONA: 3, 4, 13, 19, 21, 22

CALIFORNIA: 3, 4, 7, 8, 19, 21, 22, 24

MAINE: 4, 11, 20, 21, 22

MICHIGAN: 4, 7, 15, 20, 21, 22, 23

NEBRASKA: 3, 4, 11, 12, 16, 22, 25

NEVADA: 4, 6, 9, 11, 22

NEW JERSEY: 2, 3, 11, 12, 17, 18, 22

NEW YORK: 3, 11, 17, 18, 19, 22, 25

OREGON: 3, 11, 19, 22, 23

PENNSYLVANIA: 4, 6, 8, 11, 12, 14, 18, 21, 22

TEXAS: 4, 10, 11, 12, 26

UTAH: 4, 5, 15, 26

WASHINGTON: 4, 12, 15, 17, 19, 21, 22, 23, 26

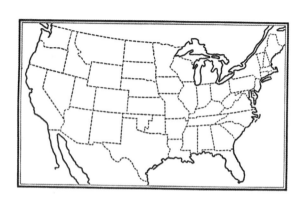

Answers on page 185.

Star Power

Fill in each of the empty squares in the grid so that each star is surrounded by the numbers 1 through 8 with no repeats.

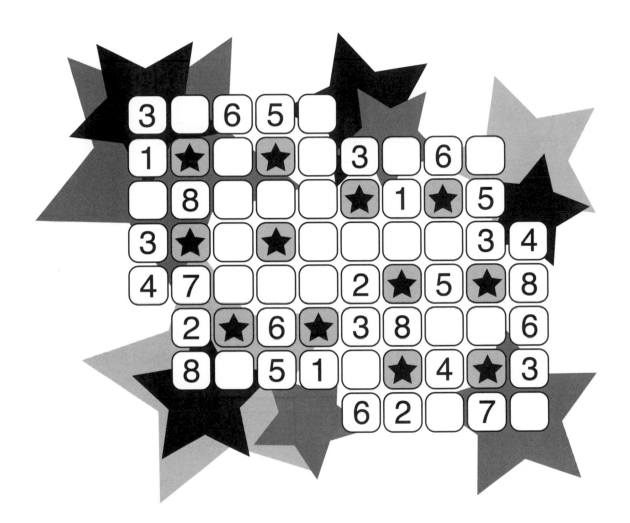

Answers on page 185.

Jersey Jumble

The 5 stars of State U's championship basketball team from 20 years ago reunited this year to play their sons, who are all members of the current State U team, in the annual father-son game. While printing the players' names on the special commemorative jerseys, the equipment manager noticed that each of the fathers had named his only son after another player on the championship team. When the equipment manager asked about it, Ed said it was his idea. He passed the idea to Smith, and then the other 3 followed suit.

The championship team was known for its trick plays, and Ed decided to help the equipment manager get the correct names on the jerseys by giving him the following trick clues: Mr. Thom's son's name is Al. Mr. Wolf's son's name is Dave. Mr. Vance named his son after Ed's dad. Mr. Unger's son is named after Bob's dad. Mr. Smith's son is named after the father of Chuck. With that information, the equipment manager printed the correct names on the jerseys, inspiring the proud dads to show their sons they still had a few more tricks up their sleeves, and they won the game. What are the first and last names of each father and his son?

Fitting Words

In this miniature crossword, the clues are listed randomly and are numbered for convenience only. It is up to you to figure out the placement of the 9 answers. To help you out, we've inserted one letter in the grid, and this is the only occurrence of that letter in the puzzle.

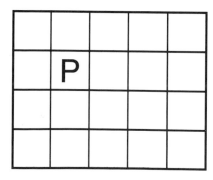

CLUES
1. Pegs on a golf course
2. Australian buddies
3. October's birthstone
4. Adolescent
5. Leftovers meal
6. Walk through water
7. Thanksgiving tubers
8. Sleeping disorder
9. Golden rule word

Answers on page 185.

XOXO

Write either an X or an O inside each empty cell of the grid so that there is no row of 4 consecutive cells with the same letter horizontally, vertically, or diagonally.

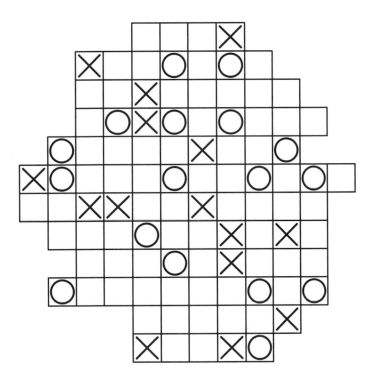

Trivia on the Brain

The ancient Egyptians regarded the brain as an unimportant organ. It was discarded during the embalming process, even as other organs (most importantly, the heart) were preserved by mummification.

Answers on page 185.

A Little Bit of Everything

GENERAL KNOWLEDGE   LANGUAGE

1	2	3	4		5	6	7	8		9	10	11
12					13					14		
15				16						17		
		18						19	20			
21	22			23			24		25			
26				27			28					
29			30							31	32	
		33							34			
35	36				37				38			
39				40		41			42			
43				44	45						46	47
48				49					50			
51				52					53			

ACROSS

1. Bar tallies
5. Included in an e-mail
9. Middle of a game
12. The rain in Spain
13. River connected to the Tiber by a canal
14. Org. with TKOs
15. Relative of Old Man Winter?
17. "Son of," to a Saudi
18. Something to play for
19. Beast of Borden
21. Pool stick
23. Part of a 3-piece suit
25. News for a gossip columnist
26. Poop deck's place
27. Chef's creations
29. "Lions for Lambs" director
33. Closes back up
34. Dijon dissent
35. Go under
37. Get under the skin of
38. Seventh out of 24, Greek-style
39. Midlife crisis symptom

41. Brother on "Frasier"
43. _____ voce (with one voice)
44. Reels from a punch
48. Homer's neighbor
49. Land measure
50. Cream, for one
51. Bunyan's tool
52. "Star Trek" actor Tim
53. Singer-songwriter Tori

DOWN

1. Muslim's cap
2. Muslim general, especially in Turkey
3. Old firefighting method
4. Samurai's quaff
5. Many a builder
6. Athletic shoes
7. Lowest commissioned rank in U.S. Navy (abbr.)
8. Shower fondness
9. Is coercive
10. Angie's role on "Law & Order"
11. "Cave _____!" ("Beware of the dog!")
16. High temperatures
20. Willingly
21. Word after used or touring
22. Visiting alien vessel
24. Climbers for creepers

28. Old Fords
30. Swimmers with toxic blood
31. Deteriorate
32. Chain material
35. Animal wildlife
36. Take over, as territory
40. Nicholas II was the last one
42. "Tell Mama" singer James
45. Old French coin
46. A "Road" picture destination for Bob and Bing
47. Urgent cry for help

Answers on page 185.

Find the Word

Ignoring spaces, capitalization, and punctuation, find all 15 occurrences of the consecutive letters H-A-N-D-Y in the paragraph below.

Sandwich Andy ran a sandwich and yogurt stand that you couldn't get a seat in at lunchtime. As a youth, Andy planned to play pro tennis, but he had a backhand you could return handily. Andy's friend Khan dyed afghan dashikis for the waiters, and Margoh, Andy's girlfriend, cooked soup made from matzoh and yummy chicken. Sandwich Andy decorated his stand with cartoons from his favorite books, *Winnie the Pooh* and *Yertle the Turtle*. Sandwich Andy planned to hand the stand to his friend Randy, a handyman who thought it was better to be disinterested than dyslexic. An orphan dying to understand sandwiches, Randy handled the fish and yellow mustard departments and proved to be handy.

Number Crossword

Fill in this crossword with numbers instead of letters. Use the clues to determine which of the numbers 1 through 9 belongs in each square. No zeros are used.

ACROSS

1. An even number
4. 1-Across plus 3-Down
5. A prime number
6. The sum of its digits is 7
7. Consecutive digits, ascending
9. Consecutive odd digits, descending

DOWN

1. A multiple of 3
2. Four different digits
3. Its middle digit is the sum of its first and last digits
4. 4-Across minus 10
5. The square of 5-Across
8. The sum of its digits is 13

Answers on pages 185–186.

Home Office Havoc

Working from home sounded like a good idea at first, but then work and home met, and the two worlds exploded. Can you find the 24 differences between these 2 messy desks?

Answers on page 186.

Amusement Park by Alpha Sleuth™

GENERAL KNOWLEDGE

LANGUAGE

PLANNING

Move each of the letters below into the grid to form common words. You will use each letter only once. The letters in the numbered cells of the grid correspond to the letters in the phrase below the grid. Completing the grid will help you complete the phrase, and vice versa. When finished, the grid and phrase should be filled with valid words, and you will have used all the letters in the letter set. The letters already included in the grid will help get you started.

HINT: The numbered cells in the grid are arranged alphabetically, so the letter in the cell marked 1 will appear in the alphabet before the letter in the cell marked 2, and so on.

A B C D E F G H I J K L M N O P Q R S T U V W X Y Z

Answers on page 186.

Red, White, Blue, and Green

Each row, column, and corner-to-corner diagonal contains 2 red squares, 2 white squares, 2 blue squares, and 2 green squares. Can you complete the grid with the clues below?

	A	B	C	D	E	F	G	H
1								
2								
3								
4								
5								
6								
7								
8								

ROW HINTS

1. Each blue is immediately right of each green; each white is immediately left of each red.
2. Both the greens are directly enclosed by a red and a blue.
4. The pattern of colors takes the form abcdacbd.
6. Two whites, a red, and a blue are directly enclosed by both the greens.
7. Each white is immediately left of each green.
8. The blues are adjacent.

COLUMN HINTS

A. Two blues, 2 whites, and a green are directly enclosed by both the reds.
B. Two whites and a green are directly enclosed by both the blues.
C. There are no greens in cells 1, 2, 3, or 4.
D. The reds are adjacent.
E. The whites are separated by 6 cells.
F. The blues are adjacent.
G. The blues are adjacent; the reds are separated by 2 cells.
H. The whites are separated by 5 cells.

Trivia on the Brain

Archaeological evidence suggests that people practiced a primitive form of brain surgery as early as 2000 B.C.

Answers on page 186.

Go Figure

COMPUTATION   **LOGIC**

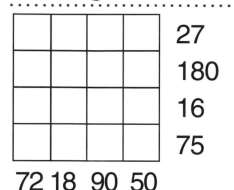

27
180
16
75

72 18 90 50

Fill each square in the grid with a digit from 1 through 6, but use only one 1 in each row and column. When the numbers in each row are multiplied, you should arrive at the total in the right-hand column. When the numbers in each column are multiplied, you should arrive at the total on the bottom line.

Word Circle

LANGUAGE   **PLANNING**

Complete the 6-letter words so the last 2 letters of the first word are the first 2 letters of the second word, and the last 2 letters of the second word are the first 2 letters of the third word, etc. The last 2 letters of the final word are the first 2 letters of the first word, thus completing the circle.

_ _ O R _ _

_ _ S T _ _

_ _ I C _ _

_ _ G A _ _

_ _ M B _ _

_ _ L U _ _

_ _ F L _ _

_ _ C I _ _

_ _ X I _ _

Answers on page 186.

Level 4

Acrostic Clues

Solve the clues below and then place the letters in their corresponding spots in the grid to reveal a quote. The letter in the upper-right corner of each grid square refers to the clue the letter comes from.

1 B	■	2 D	3 G	4 I	■	5 H	6 A	7 H	8 A	9 F	10 H	11 B	■	12 C	13 I			
14 D	15 D	16 E	17 D	■	18 C	19 F	20 A	21 G	22 F	23 D	24 A	25 D	26 F	27 H	28 C			
29 G	30 A	31 A	32 B	33 A	■	34 E	35 B	■	36 C	37 D	38 F	39 I	■	40 E	41 A	42 F		
43 E	44 E	45 E	■	46 H	47 C	48 H	49 F	50 H	51 I	52 E	■	53 I	54 I	■	55 C	56 H	57 C	58 B
59 D	60 A	61 A	62 I	■	63 G	■	64 F	65 A	66 A	67 H	68 G	69 F	70 I	71 A				
72 B	73 A	74 A	75 G	76 H	77 B	78 C	79 H	80 E	81 B	82 D								

A. Author of quote (2 words)

— — — — — — — — — — — — — — —
(71) (41) (66) (33) (30) (74) (73) (24) (6) (31) (65) (8) (60) (61) (20)

B. James _____ Cooper

— — — — — — — —
(35) (11) (77) (1) (32) (81) (72) (58)

C. Andalusian dance

— — — — — — — —
(57) (55) (78) (36) (28) (12) (18) (47)

D. Burial alternative

— — — — — — — — —
(2) (23) (17) (14) (25) (59) (37) (15) (82)

E. Ruby anniversary

— — — — — — — —
(40) (34) (16) (43) (80) (45) (52) (44)

F. Legendary thief (2 words)

— — — — — — — — —
(42) (22) (26) (9) (38) (64) (19) (69) (49)

G. Illicit liaison

— — — — — —
(63) (29) (21) (3) (75) (68)

H. Immunizing

— — — — — — — — — — —
(56) (10) (67) (46) (50) (27) (7) (79) (5) (48) (76)

I. Befuddle

— — — — — — — —
(51) (13) (4) (54) (53) (70) (62) (39)

Answers on page 186.

Sudoku

		3	2		7			
					3	1		9
1					6	4		
3						6	1	
			5					
	8	7						5
		4	1					7
2		8	4					
			8		2	3		

Use deductive logic to complete the grid so that each row, each column, and each 3 by 3 box contains the numbers 1 through 9 in some order. The solution is unique.

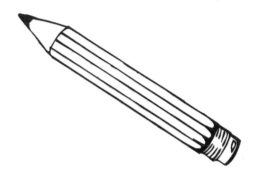

Hinky Pinky

The clues below lead to a 2-word answer that rhymes, such as Big Pig or Stable Table. The numbers in parentheses after the clue give the number of syllables in each word.

1. Talent with a tool (1): _____
2. Arrive at last at the seashore (1): _____
3. Blamed the trouble on a type of shake (2): _____
4. Bother the court entertainer (2): _____
5. Persistent interest in the invasion and control of a foreign nation for a second time (5): _____

Answers on pages 186–187.

Word Columns

Find the hidden phrase by using the letters directly below each of the blank squares.
Each letter is used only once.

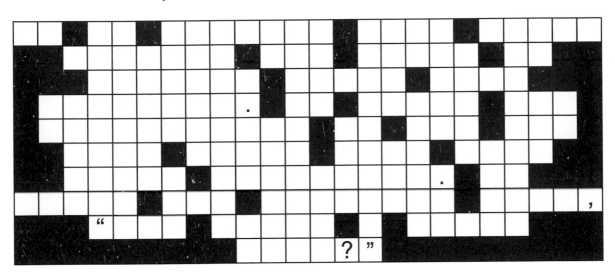

```
                    n
         l        r       e       a              e
      i  s     a  a   r o l    a   h         t
      s  o c i u E t a t h    o s r e       m
      u  i s c r n m o t h p  b n k z d o h f
      e  m s t h e a i c u t t g o s m s c o i
   t  s  t x i y m s b o o t w s h C i i I h h d
   a  n  e H e w i n g r H e e i r a t x B t a b
I  R  o  p h o h a s u g e e e t t f e e r o e e
s  e  F  s s a r i t m o c d e a s a w d t h b s y
```

Answers on page 187.

All Mixed Up

GENERAL KNOWLEDGE

LANGUAGE

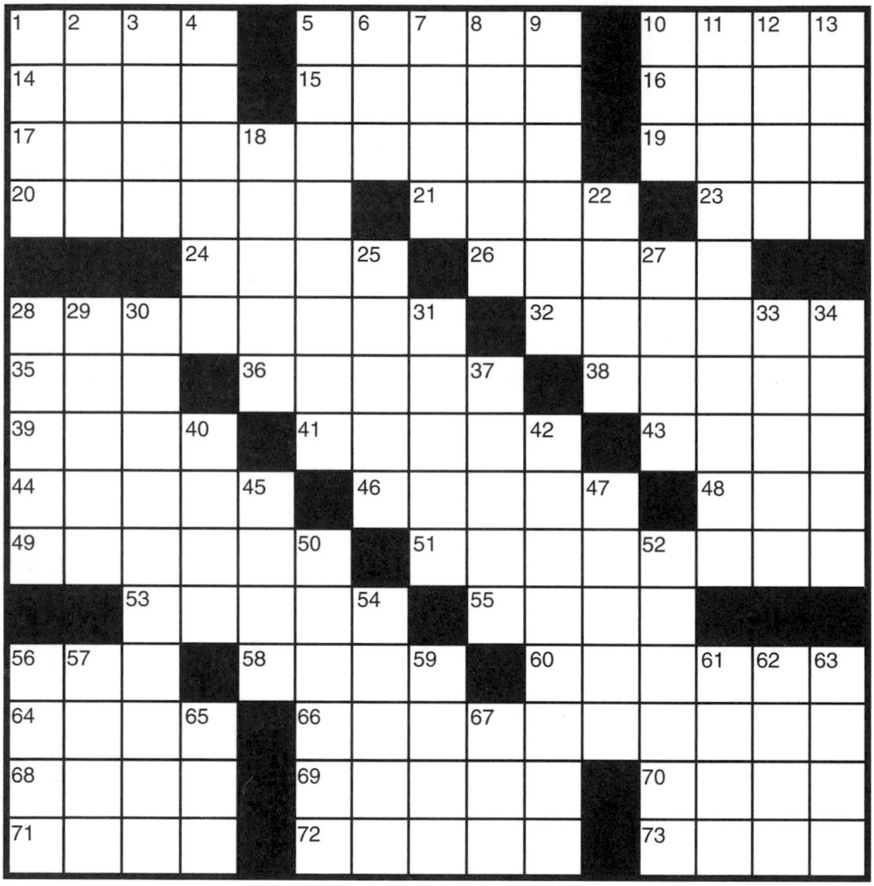

ACROSS

1. Kind of list
5. Pasta topper
10. Fence the goods, say
14. Moonfish
15. Forearm bones
16. Lose brightness
17. Aviator pleads?
19. Forest unit
20. Said it wasn't so
21. Salty septet
23. Terminus
24. Orch. section
26. Bombing on stage
28. "Slammin'" golf legend
32. Prepares clams, perhaps
35. Turkish honorific
36. Music-maker's org.
38. Whom Bugs bugs
39. Hound sound

41. Bush
43. Light tune
44. Offer one's 2 cents
46. "Like a Rock" rocker
48. Museum-funding org.
49. Domingo and others
51. Alcoves
53. Leaves
55. Meter maid leavings: abbr.
56. Massages elicit them
58. A pop
60. Many John Wayne movies
64. Anger, and then some
66. 17-Across, 11-Down, and 30-Down—all mixed up
68. [Sigh]
69. Thrusting weapon
70. Speak with vitriol
71. Flappers' hairdos
72. Urged, with "on"
73. Certain NCOs

DOWN

1. Swamp critter
2. Mayberry kid
3. "Aw, heck!"
4. "Excuse me, waitress?"
5. Summer outfit
6. Priest's robe
7. French articles
8. Like some parrots
9. University application parts
10. Toward the stern
11. Naked urchins?
12. First place?
13. Prepared for driving

18. Insurance giant
22. Location
25. Goldman's partner on Wall Street
27. "Little" Dickens girl
28. Wooden shoe
29. Wide open
30. Leathernecks chat?
31. Risk-taker
33. Free-for-all
34. Puerto Rican misses: abbr.
37. Washington's _____ Sound
40. Fort with a fortune
42. Summoned
45. Buffalo's lake
47. Change the price, maybe
50. Horse home
52. Cool red giants in the sky
54. Scrawny one
56. Swift, compact horse
57. Heavenly overhead?
59. Suspend
61. Online periodical
62. Monthly payment for some
63. Retired jets: abbr.
65. Slalom curve
67. Cooler contents

Answers on page 187.

The Bicker Prize

The judges are about to announce the order of the prizewinners at the Bicker Prize awards for the best novel of the year. However, the records clerk has not been paying attention. Although each item is in the correct column, only 1 item in each column is correctly positioned. The following facts are certain about the correct order:

1. Jacobs is 2 places above Oasis but only 1 above Betty.

2. Nemesis is somewhere above Indigo, which is somewhere above Evelyn.

3. Amy is 2 places above Keene, which is 1 place below Rodent.

	Name	Surname	Book
1	Amy	Golem	Maddy
2	Betty	Handle	Nemesis
3	Cedric	Indigo	Oasis
4	Dennis	Jacobs	Patronage
5	Evelyn	Keene	Quanta
6	Freda	Lever	Rodent

4. Freda is somewhere above Jacobs, which is 1 place below Maddy.

5. Patronage is 2 places below Golem but only 1 above Dennis.

Can you determine the correct first name, surname, and book title for each position?

Time Well Spent

Fill in the blanks in the sentence below with 6-letter words that are anagrams (rearrangements of the same letters) of one another.

Several hours can _____ quickly if you're _____, so _____ try to stay awake.

Answers on page 187.

Star Power

Fill in each of the empty squares in the grid so that each star is surrounded by the numbers 1 through 8 with no repeats.

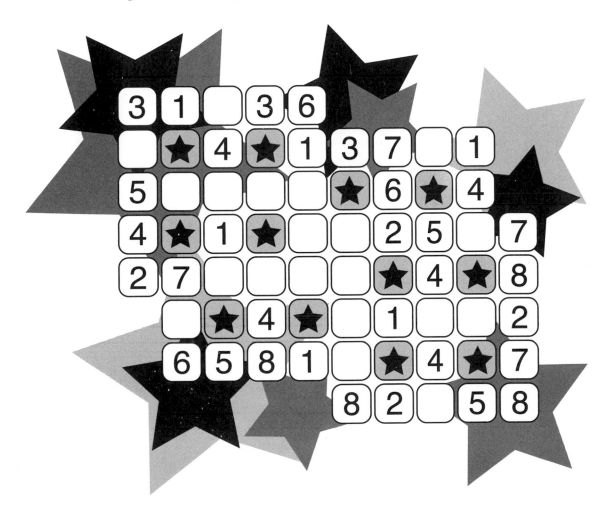

Trivia on the Brain

For a period of time between 1100 and 1500 A.D., study of the human brain ceased because of a religious ban on dissection and the study of human anatomy.

Answers on page 187.

Code-Doku

LOGIC

	L	T				P
	N					
	N				O	
	M				L	
O			L	P	M	
E		A	M			
			O			A
		N				S
S	P		A	T		

Use deductive logic to complete the grid so that each row, each column, and each 3 by 3 box contains the letters in the words PET SALMON. When you have completed the puzzle, read the shaded squares to form a phrase that describes a great feat of exploration.

A Puzzling Perspective

LANGUAGE SPATIAL VISUALIZATION

Mentally arrange the lettered balls from large to small in the correct order to spell an 11-letter word.

Clue: Patentable

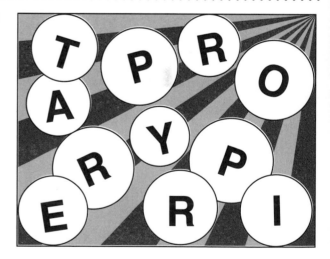

Answers on page 187.

Alien Revolution

Can you form something recognizable out of these strange shapes?

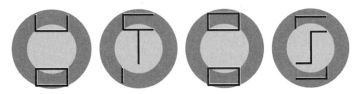

Word Ladder

Change just one letter on each line to go from the top word to the bottom word. Do not change the order of the letters. You must have a common English word at each step.

HITCH

_____

_____

_____

_____

_____

_____

_____

_____

HIKER

Answers on page 187.

Trick or Treat! by Alpha Sleuth™

GENERAL KNOWLEDGE

LANGUAGE

PLANNING

Move each of the letters below into the grid to form common words. You will use each letter only once. The letters in the numbered cells of the grid correspond to the letters in the phrase below the grid. Completing the grid will help you complete the phrase, and vice versa. When finished, the grid and phrase should be filled with valid words, and you will have used all the letters in the letter set. The letters already included in the grid will help get you started.

HINT: The numbered cells in the grid are arranged alphabetically, so the letter in the cell marked 1 will appear in the alphabet before the letter in the cell marked 2, and so on.

A B C D E F G H I J K L M N
O P Q R S T U V W X Y Z

Trivia on the Brain

A piece of your brain about the size of a grain of sand contains more than 100,000 neurons and nearly 1 billion synapses.

Answers on page 187.

Number Crossword

Fill in this crossword with numbers instead of letters. Use the clues to determine which of the numbers 1 through 9 belongs in each empty square. No zeros are used.

ACROSS

1. Consecutive digits, out of order
4. Consecutive digits, out of order
6. Its last digit is the sum of its first 3 digits
8. Consecutive even digits, descending

DOWN

1. A multiple of 18
2. Consecutive odd digits, descending
3. Consecutive even digits, out of order
5. 1-Down plus 7-Down
7. A multiple of 7

Wacky Wordy

Can you "read" the phrase below?

JUDADDGE

Trivia on the Brain

The size of an animal's brain doesn't necessarily correspond to the size of the animal. The brain of an adult great white shark weighs only 34 grams, while the brain of a baboon weighs 137 grams. A tiny newborn human baby's brain can weigh up to 400 grams!

Answers on page 188.

Sudoku

LOGIC

	7	3	6					
				3	1			
8	5				4			2
		5				4	9	
				6				
	1	2				3		
5			1				7	8
			2	7				
				3	9	4		

Use deductive logic to complete the grid so that each row, each column, and each 3 by 3 box contains the numbers 1 through 9 in some order. The solution is unique.

Birthday Party Puzzle

LOGIC

The moms in the neighborhood decided it was time for the dads to bond with their daughters, so they cooked up a birthday party for one of the girls. Four dads, each with a young daughter in tow, were at the birthday party. Although the girls knew each other from school, the dads did not know each other, nor did they know which girl

belonged to which dad and how old each girl was. The birthday girl's mom gave the men the following helpful hints: The girls are aged 5, 6, 7, and 8, and it is Jeff's daughter's birthday party. Brianna is not the oldest girl. Steve's daughter, Alicia, was 4 just over a year ago. Larry's daughter will be 7 on her next birthday. Darla is older than Carol. Tom's daughter is the oldest. Carol is older than Larry's daughter. How old is each girl, and who is each one's father?

Answers on page 188.

Keep 'Em Separated

Draw 4 lines so that 13 distinct segments, each of which contains 1 circle, exist in the square. The lines must be the same length and originate from 4 different points.

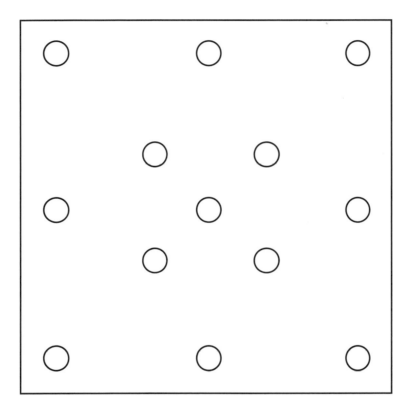

Trivia on the Brain

During the first month of life, the number of synapses in a human infant's brain increases from 50 trillion to 1 quadrillion. If the infant's body grew at a comparable rate, his weight would increase dramatically from about 8.5 pounds at birth to 170 pounds at 1 month old!

Answer on page 188.

Red, White, Blue, and Green

Each row, column, and corner-to-corner diagonal contains 2 red squares, 2 white squares, 2 blue squares, and 2 green squares. Can you complete the grid with the clues below?

	A	B	C	D	E	F	G	H
1								
2								
3								
4								
5								
6								
7								
8								

ROW HINTS

1. Each white is immediately right of each red.
2. Three different colors are directly enclosed by the reds.
3. Two whites, a blue, and a green are directly enclosed by the reds.
4. The greens are separated by 6 cells.
5. Three different colors are directly enclosed by the reds.
6. The pattern of colors takes the form abbcaddc.
7. The greens are separated by 4 cells.
8. The reds are separated by 6 cells; the greens are directly enclosed by the blues.

COLUMN HINTS

A. Two whites, 2 blues, and a green are directly enclosed by the reds.
B. Two greens, 2 blues, and a red are directly enclosed by the whites.
D. Two blues and a green are directly enclosed by the reds.
H. A blue and a white are directly enclosed by the reds.

Trivia on the Brain

It's hard to imagine, but all of your thoughts are actually produced by a combination of electricity and chemicals.

Answers on page 188.

Word Ladder

Change just one letter on each line to go from the top word to the bottom word. Do not change the order of the letters. You must have a common English word at each step.

WHEAT

_____

_____

_____

_____

_____

FLOUR

A Puzzling Perspective

Mentally arrange the lettered balls from large to small in the correct order to spell an 11-letter word.

Clue: Ponderously clumsy

Answers on page 188.

Manly Names

GENERAL KNOWLEDGE | LANGUAGE

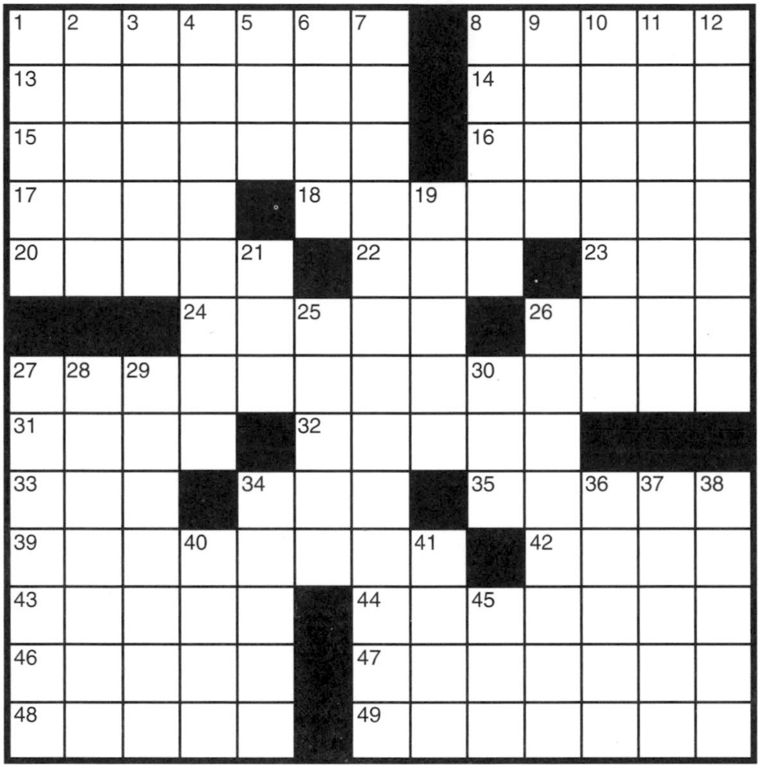

ACROSS

1. Dodge traffic, perhaps
8. Narrow estuary
13. Momentum
14. Goodbye, maybe
15. South American hero
16. Three-masted ship
17. "Monday Night Football" network
18. Old stereo component
20. Classroom sights
22. Pennington and Cobb
23. Cambodian currency
24. Vieira's cohost
26. Boot base
27. Befitting a blackguard
31. Paella ingredient
32. One member of Houston's NFL team
33. Bird with a snood
34. Foot, to Flavius
35. Leia strangled him

39. Small, as a town
42. Like many basketball players
43. Devonshire dad
44. A number that designates place
46. Patronized a certain restaurant
47. State of perfect inner peace
48. Finds peace
49. Scanner dial

DOWN

1. Sudden shift while sailing
2. Narrow winning margin
3. Short shouts
4. Dermal features
5. Off-road ride: abbr.
6. Bloody Mary's daughter
7. Mr. Miyagi's gift to Daniel
8. Documents sent by phone
9. "_____ Three Lives"
10. Actor Paul in the College Football Hall of Fame
11. Jennifer Lopez movie
12. High-stepping horse
19. Corning glass
21. _____ Marino
25. Speak
26. Having healing powers
27. At an acceptable level
28. Recent delivery

29. Oogenesis products
30. Capt.'s superior
34. Where cables connect
36. Uninspiring
37. Maillot _____ (Tour de France jersey for younger competitors)
38. Sufism deity
40. Preliminary race
41. "Coming to America" actor La Salle
45. _____ Hill (music group)

Answers on page 188.

Code-Doku

LOGIC

			O			
	K	O			B		S
	B	K					Y
U					A	K
S	A			U		
		U	B		C	
	S		K	R		O
A	C		S			

Use deductive logic to complete the grid so that each row, each column, and each 3 by 3 box contains the letters in the words A ROSY BUCK. When you have completed the puzzle, read the shaded squares to describe something you might see at the beach.

XX Marks This Spot

ANALYSIS CREATIVE THINKING

Determine the next number in this progression.

38978567796588__?

Answers on page 188.

Fitting Words

In this miniature crossword, the clues are listed randomly and are numbered for convenience only. It is up to you to figure out the placement of the 9 answers. To help you out, we've inserted one letter in the grid, and this is the only occurrence of that letter in the puzzle.

CLUES

1. Goes limp
2. Web destination
3. Strike zone's lower boundary
4. Run in neutral
5. Mill input
6. Rubberneck
7. _____ and turn
8. Sound portion of a broadcast
9. Archaeologist's workplace, sometimes

Hinky Pinky

The clues below lead to a 2-word answer that rhymes, such as Big Pig or Stable Table. The numbers in parentheses after the clue give the number of syllables in each word.

1. Once-a-year-issued car owner's reference booklet (3): _____

2. Affected behavior during an after-school punishment session (3): _____

3. Feeling of thankfulness for having leeway to act (3): _____

4. Close examination of a shipboard rebellion (3): _____

5. Statute violator's slow-dissolving candy (3): _____

Answers on page 188.

Acrostic Clues

Solve the clues below and then place the letters in their corresponding spots in the grid to reveal a quote by a famous person. The letter in the upper-right corner of each grid square refers to the clue the letter comes from.

1 G		2 J	3 D	4 I	5 E	6 A		7 I	8 C	9 E	10 A	11 G	12 B	13 D	14 G			15 C	16 A
17 C	18 I	19 E		20 E	21 J	22 H		23 B	24 B	25 E		26 D	27 E	28 G	29 I				
30 A	31 A	32 I	33 A	34 A		35 A	36 E	37 G	38 A	39 B		40 F	41 B	42 I					
43 H	44 F	45 E	46 B	47 I	48 A	49 H	50 H	51 D		52 B	53 F		54 F	55 F	56 J				
57 H	58 G	59 B	60 B	61 D	62 F		63 H	64 H	65 G	66 C		67 G	68 J		69 G	70 F	71 D	72 G	73 J

A. Author of quote (2 words)

___ ___ ___ ___ ___ ___ ___ ___ ___ ___
(35) (31) (33) (38) (6) (16) (30) (10) (48) (34)

B. Renounced

___ ___ ___ ___ ___ ___ ___ ___ ___
(24) (46) (39) (52) (60) (59) (12) (41) (23)

C. Charon's river

___ ___ ___ ___
(17) (15) (66) (8)

D. Removed dandelions

___ ___ ___ ___ ___ ___
(26) (3) (61) (51) (13) (71)

E. Novice or fledgling

___ ___ ___ ___ ___ ___ ___ ___
(45) (5) (36) (9) (27) (25) (20) (19)

F. Type of wedding?

___ ___ ___ ___ ___ ___ ___
(62) (55) (70) (54) (40) (44) (53)

G. Clarified

___ ___ ___ ___ ___ ___ ___ ___ ___ ___
(65) (58) (37) (11) (1) (67) (72) (69) (28) (14)

H. King or Hawking

___ ___ ___ ___ ___ ___ ___
(43) (63) (50) (57) (64) (22) (49)

I. Project or undertaking

___ ___ ___ ___ ___ ___ ___
(4) (18) (29) (42) (47) (32) (7)

J. Sugar alternative

___ ___ ___ ___ ___
(21) (68) (2) (56) (73)

Answers on page 189.

Word Jigsaw

Fit the pieces into the frame to form common, uncapitalized words reading across and down crossword-style. There's no need to rotate the pieces; they'll fit as shown, with each piece used exactly once.

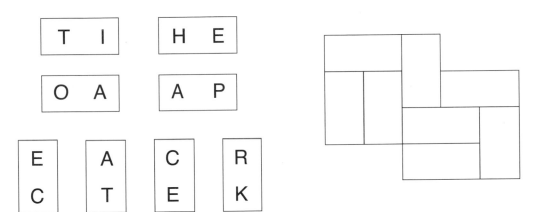

Number Noggin-Scratcher (Part 1)

Look at the list of numerals below for 1 minute, and then turn the page.

29751036497521639582

Answers on page 189.

Number Noggin-Scratcher (Part 2) MEMORY

(Do not read this until you have read the previous page!)

Which one of the following groups of 3 numbers is repeated in the sequence?

A. 364   B. 975   C. 958   D. 649   E. 497

Number Crossword COMPUTATION LOGIC

Fill in this crossword with numbers instead of letters. Use the clues to determine which number from 1 through 9 belongs in each empty square. No zeros are used.

ACROSS
1. A square number
4. Consecutive digits, descending
5. Its last digit is the sum of its first 4 digits
6. A power of 2
7. A multiple of 77

DOWN
1. Consecutive odd digits, out of order
2. A palindrome
3. Its digits sum is 20
4. Its last digit is the sum of its first 3 digits
5. An even number

Trivia on the Brain
The ancient philosopher Aristotle believed that the organ of sensation and thought was the heart. The brain, he claimed, was merely an instrument designed to cool it.

Answers on page 189.

Star Power

Fill in each of the empty squares in the grid so that each star is surrounded by the numbers 1 through 8 with no repeats.

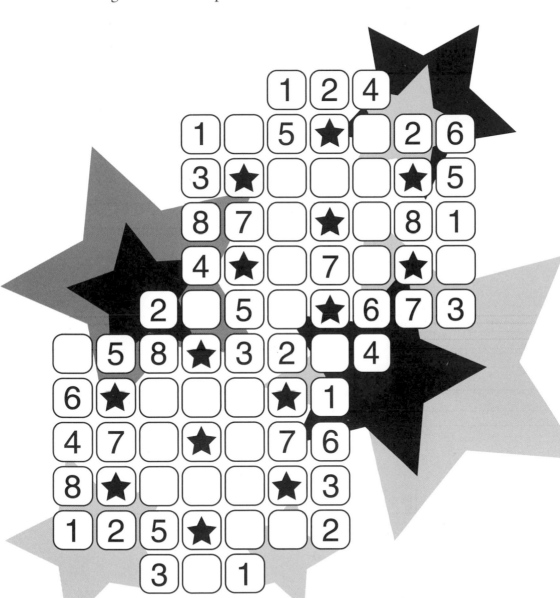

Answers on page 189.

Scramblegram U.S. Tour

GENERAL KNOWLEDGE   **LANGUAGE**

Four 11-letter words, all of which revolve around the same theme, have been jumbled. Unscramble the 4 words and write the answers in the space next to each one. Next, transfer the letters that are in the shaded boxes into the empty spaces below and unscramble the 9-letter word that goes with the theme. The theme for this puzzle is U.S. cities.

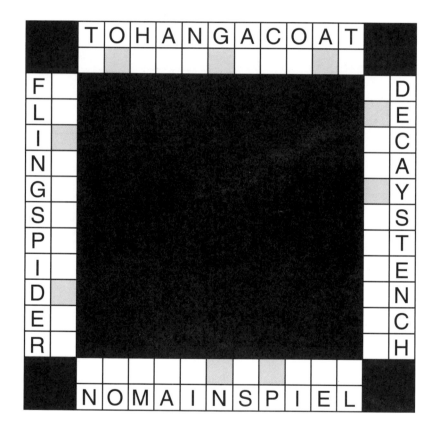

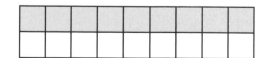

Answers on page 189.

Sudoku

Use deductive logic to complete the grid so that each row, each column, and each 3 by 3 box contains the numbers 1 through 9 in some order. The solution is unique.

		7		9	8		2	
	8		6					7
1		3	2				4	
	5			4			1	
	2				7	3		6
5					4		8	
	6		3	7		4		

Stadium Improvements

Fill in the blanks in the sentence below with 6-letter words that are anagrams (rearrangements of the same letters) of one another.

Word _____ quickly that the San Diego _____ had _____ no expense in furnishing all of the skyboxes with brand-new _____.

Answers on page 189.

Word Columns

Find the hidden quote by using the letters directly below each of the blank squares.
Each letter is used only once.

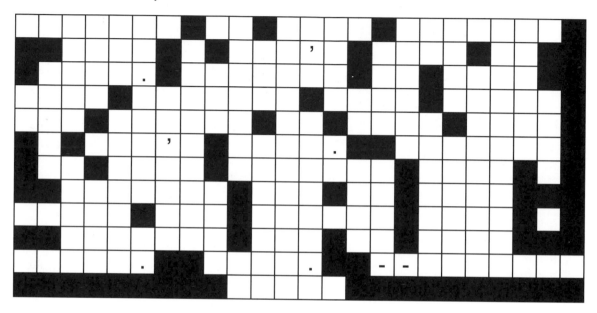

```
                        a
                        o                                   o
      o    t            t  g                          n    o    t
      e    d    t    P    me  o    m                  k    d    t
  b   e    n    e    n    e  r    k  n    o    r    s    D    h    w    e
  b   o    h    f    c    i  m    d  e    n    n    w    n    k    g    k    n    r    t    r    a
  m   d    e    w    i    d  e    d  A    n    f    i    o    t    o    o    w    h    a    w    l    I
P r   o    u    o    h    n  n    m  s    d    e    t    s    h    a    k    n    f    h    g    n    g
a I   n    t    c    i    t  t    w  o    t    o    c    t    g    n    P    e    o    t    e    o    e
a k   e    e    c    k    d  I    A  k    n    n    w    t    t    n    e    t    o    o    w    a    t
a v   w    o    a    t    o  o    g  d    o    h    t    i    n    o    e    r    t    u    h    c    t
e r   d    u    t    r    t  h    e  i    n    t    o    t    m    m    t    t    o    a    i    m    I    s
```

Answers on page 189.

Get It Straight

Don't get too caught up in all the twists and turns as you negotiate your way to the center of this intricate labyrinth.

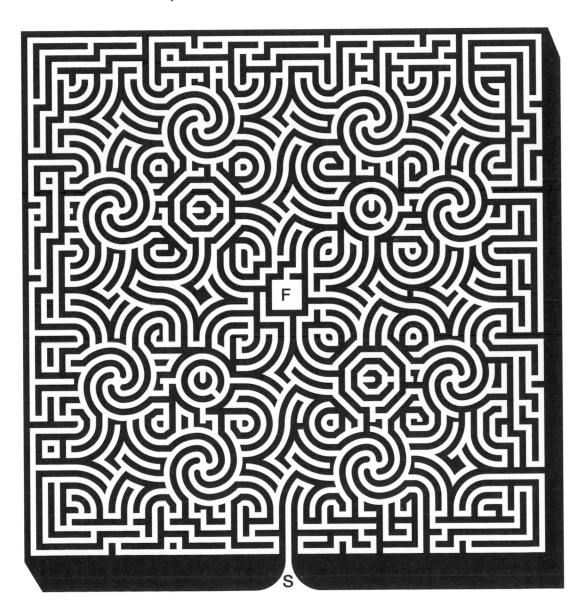

Answer on page 190.

Mail Service

ACROSS

1. Achieve through deception
8. Native Israeli
13. "Told you so"
14. Really dug
15. Chump
16. Smiling
17. _____ Conner, Miss USA 2006
18. Seemed likely
20. Tonto's horse
22. Wade opponent
23. Emergency med. procedure
24. Sings the praises of
26. Obligation
27. Business address, perhaps
31. Parliamentary procedures?
32. Hubbub

33. KITT or General Lee
34. New Deal monogram
35. Emulated a sous chef
39. Tree carvings
42. Malcolm Arnold's "Fantasy for Cello," for example
43. Fabrications
44. Best possible
46. Latin clarifier
47. Childlike attitude
48. Gives off, as light
49. Met at the door

DOWN

1. Partner of figures
2. Violinist Stern
3. Part of TNT
4. Attacks
5. Disparity
6. Tale-teller
7. "American History X" star
8. Noncom's nickname
9. Plugging away
10. Den denizen
11. Approach quickly
12. Bird in "B.C."
19. Polite refusal
21. Chinese ideal
25. Norwegian "ouch"

26. Putting down
27. Promoting peace
28. National anthem since 1980
29. Three make a turkey
30. Potential bait-taker
34. Bruce Lee's weapons
36. Doomsday cause, perhaps
37. Fill with happiness
38. Handed (out)
40. Experiment
41. Category of crystals
45. Casual Friday omission

Answers on page 190.

Put Your Intellect in Overdrive

Word Ladder

LANGUAGE   PLANNING

Change just one letter on each line to go from the top word to the bottom word. Do not change the order of the letters. You must have a word at each step.

CEDAR

_____

_____

_____

_____

_____

_____

_____

_____

_____

_____

CHEST

Rounders

ANALYSIS

Which one of the figures doesn't belong?

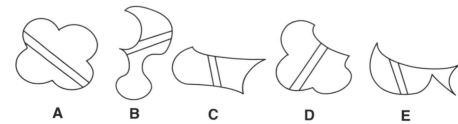

A   B   C   D   E

Answers on page 190.

160

Name Calling

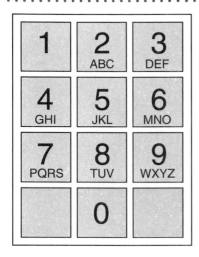

Decipher the encoded word in the quip below using the numbers and letters on the phone pad. Remember that each number can stand for 3 or 4 possible letters.

It's kind of fun to do the 4–6–7–6–7–7–4–2–5–3.

Memory Mishmash (Part 1)

Study the grid below for 3 minutes, and then turn the page.

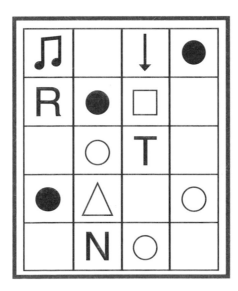

Answers on page 190.

Memory Mishmash (Part 2)

(Do not read this until you have read the previous page!)

1. How many white circles does the grid contain? _____

2. Which letter appears beneath the triangle? _____

3. The arrow is pointing to which geometric figure? _____

4. Which symbol appears in the top left-hand corner? _____

5. How many black circles appear in the grid? _____

6. The letter T appears to the right of which geometric figure? _____

7. Which letter appears in the second row? _____

Fitting Words

In this miniature crossword, the clues are listed randomly and are numbered for convenience only. It is up to you to figure out the placement of the 9 answers. To help you out, we've inserted one letter in the grid, and this is the only occurrence of that letter in the puzzle.

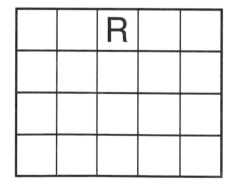

CLUES
1. Destiny
2. Gibbons and gorillas
3. Frat party containers
4. Smooths wood
5. Bankruptcy
6. Cunning
7. Cheddar choice
8. Blue hue
9. Furnish

Answers on page 190.

Creature Feature by Alpha Sleuth™

Move each of the letters below into the grid to form common words. You will use each letter only once. The letters in the numbered cells of the grid correspond to the letters in the phrase below the grid. Completing the grid will help you complete the phrase, and vice versa. When finished, the grid and phrase should be filled with valid words, and you will have used all the letters in the letter set. The letters already included in the grid will help get you started.

HINT: The numbered cells in the grid are arranged alphabetically, so the letter in the cell marked 1 will appear in the alphabet before the letter in the cell marked 2, and so on.

A B C D E F G H I J K L M N O P Q R S T U V W X Y Z

	1	8	4	7	1	6	
2	9	1	2	5	3	9	10

Trivia on the Brain

Each of your eyes contains 3 million cone cells that are sensitive to color. Think that's a lot? Each of your eyes also contains 100 million cells that are sensitive to light!

Answers on page 190.

Strings Attached

The words in all capital letters are anagrams (rearrangements of the same letters) of things that contain strings. Can you work out all these knots?

"Gather 'round, friends!" said the teacher at the Institute of String Theory. "Here's your challenge: think of something that has strings, and then form it into an anagram. Who wants to go first?"

"How about SCARLET CAD, a kid's game?" one young genius piped up.

"I have one," a girl in a blue sweater said. "SOPHIE FLING, something you can use to catch a whopper—maybe."

"TRAINEE TOM, something you can make dance," another girl offered.

"ANCIENT TREKS, something you can use on a court," a jock in a letter sweater said.

"TOE BOIL," said another. "It looks better than it sounds!"

"I have no idea what it's for, but a BLIMP LUNE can help you go straight," a student remarked.

"DAMN LION!" a girl yelled. "I mean, pardon my language, but it does make a nice sound."

Answers on page 190.

Get It Straight

Don't get too caught up in all the twists and turns as you negotiate your way to the center of this intricate labyrinth.

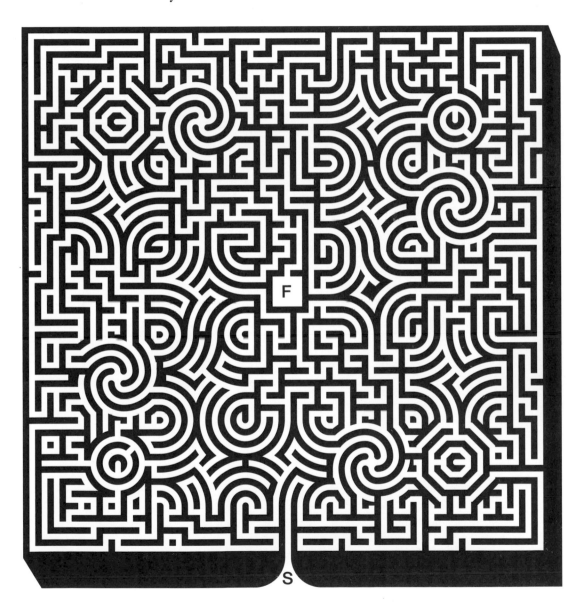

Answer on page 190.

Red, White, Blue, and Green

Each row, column, and corner-to-corner diagonal contains 2 red squares, 2 white squares, 2 blue squares, and 2 green squares. Can you complete the grid with the clues below?

	A	B	C	D	E	F	G	H
1								
2								
3								
4								
5								
6								
7								
8								

ROW HINTS

2. The reds are adjacent.
3. The whites cannot be found in cells A, B, C, or D.
5. The blues are separated by 6 cells.
6. The reds are adjacent; each green is immediately right of each blue.
8. The pattern of colors takes the form abaccbdd.

COLUMN HINTS

A. The greens are separated by 6 cells; each blue is directly above each red.
B. Three different colors are directly enclosed by the whites.
D. One blue is directly enclosed by the greens.
F. Each white is directly above each green.
G. The whites cannot be found in cells 5, 6, 7, or 8; each blue is directly above each red.
H. Two greens and a red are directly enclosed by the blues.

Trivia on the Brain

A person dreams, on average, about 4 or 5 times each night. Yet rarely do we remember having dreamed at all!

Answers on page 190.

REASSESS YOUR BRAIN

You have just completed a set of puzzles selected to challenge your various mental skills. We hope you enjoyed them. And did the mental exercise you engaged in also improve your memory, attention, problem solving and other important cognitive skills? In order to find out, please fill out this questionnaire. It is exactly the same as the one you filled out before you embarked on our puzzles. So now you will be in a position to compare your cognitive skills before and after you challenged them with cognitive exercise. The real question is whether solving our puzzles had a real impact on your real-life performance; we hope it did.

The questions below are designed to test your skills in the areas of memory, problem solving, creative thinking, attention, language, and more. Please reflect on each question, and rate your abilities on a 5-point scale, where 5 equals "excellent" and 1 equals "very poor." Then tally up your scores, and check out the categories at the bottom of the next page to learn how you have sharpened your brain.

1. You get a new cell phone. How long does it take you to remember the number? Give yourself a 1 if you have to check the phone every time you want to give out the number, and a 5 if you know it by heart the next day.

1   2   3   4   5

2. How good are you at remembering where you put things? Give yourself a 5 if you never lose anything, but a 1 if you have to search for the keys every time you want to leave the house.

1   2   3   4   5

3. You have a busy work day that you've carefully planned around a doctor's appointment. At the last minute, the doctor's office calls and asks you to reschedule your appointment from afternoon to morning. How good are you at juggling your plans to accommodate this change?

1   2   3   4   5

4. You're taking a trip back to your hometown, and have several old friends to see, as well as old haunts to visit. You'll only be there for three days. How good are you at planning your visit so you can accomplish everything?

1   2   3   4   5

5. A friend takes you to the opera, and the next morning a curious coworker wants to hear the plot in depth. How good are you at remembering all the details?

1   2   3   4   5

6. You're brokering an agreement between two parties, and each party keeps changing their demands. How good are you at adapting to the changing situation?

1   2   3   4   5

7. You're cooking a big meal for a family celebration. You have to cook everything—appetizers, entrees, sides, and desserts—all on the same day. How good are you at planning out each recipe so that everything is done and you can sit down and enjoy the meal with your family?

1   2   3   4   5

8. In an emotionally charged situation (for example, when you're giving a toast), can you usually come up with the right words to describe your feelings?

1   2   3   4   5

9. You and 5 friends have made a vow to always spend a certain amount of money on each other for holiday gifts. How good are you at calculating the prices of things in your head to make sure you spend the right amount of money?

1   2   3   4   5

10. You're moving, and you have to coordinate all the details of packing, hiring movers, cutting off and setting up utilities, and a hundred other small details. How good are you at planning out this complex situation?

1   2   3   4   5

10–25 Points:
Are You Ready to Make a Change?
Keep at it: There are plenty of activities that will help you improve your brain health! Continue working puzzles on a regular basis. Pick up another *Brain Games*™ book, and choose a different type of puzzle each day, or do a variety of them daily to help strengthen memory, focus attention, and improve logic and problem solving.

26–40 Points:
Building Your Mental Muscle
You're no mental slouch, but there's always room to sharpen your mind! Try to identify the types of puzzles that you found particularly difficult in this book. Then you'll get an idea of which cognitive skills you need to work on. Remember, doing a puzzle can be the mental equivalent of doing lunges or squats: While they might not be your first choice of activity, you'll definitely like the results!

41–50 Points:
View from the Top
Congratulations! You have finished the puzzles in this book and are performing like a champion. To maintain this level of mental fitness, keep challenging yourself by working puzzles every day. Like the rest of the body's muscles, your mental strength can decline if you don't use it. So choose to keep your brain strong and active. You're at the summit—now you just have to stay to enjoy the view!

ANSWERS

Sudoku (page 11)

5	7	3	8	6	1	9	2	4
2	6	9	3	4	7	5	8	1
1	8	4	2	9	5	3	7	6
3	5	1	9	7	6	2	4	8
6	4	8	5	3	2	7	1	9
7	9	2	4	1	8	6	5	3
8	1	7	6	2	9	4	3	5
9	3	5	7	8	4	1	6	2
4	2	6	1	5	3	8	9	7

Go Figure (page 11)

			75
6	4	5	120
4	5	6	120
3	1	2	6

72 20 60 60

A Matter of Time (pages 12–13)

W	A	I	T	E		T	S	P		O	A	F
A	N	N	E	X		E	P	A		H	M	O
S	T	A	M	P		S	A	S	S	I	E	R
		S	P	L	I	T	S	E	C	O	N	D
S	I	T	S	O	N		M	O	O			
C	S	A		I	C	Y		R	O	A	M	
U	P	T	O	T	H	E	M	I	N	U	T	E
D	Y	E	R		W	O	N		T	V	S	
		A	A	A		T	H	R	A	S	H	
T	W	E	L	F	T	H	H	O	U	R		
W	E	B	S	I	T	E		U	R	G	E	S
O	N	A		R	A	W		S	A	U	T	E
S	T	Y		E	R	S		E	L	E	C	T

Hinky Pinky (page 14)

1. Poe's/hose; 2. bare/heir; 3. ditz/quits;
4. nearing/clearing; 5. charity/rarity

Wacky Wordy (page 14)

Six pack

Go Figure (page 15)

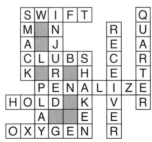

						28
9	6	2	1	4	3	25
5	2	2	4	1	7	21
3	7	6	2	3	4	25
2	4	9	5	3	1	24
1	7	2	5	4	2	21
6	1	5	4	8	3	27

26 27 26 21 23 20 29

But Who Controlled the Radio? (page 15)

Marsha drove 30 miles more than John did. If X represents the entire distance, then Marsha drove $65 + (X - 50)$, which simplifies to $(X + 15)$ miles. John drove $(X - 65) + 50$, which simplifies to $(X - 15)$ miles. The difference between $(X + 15)$ and $(X - 15)$ is 30 miles.

Acrostic Clues (page 16)

A. Thomas Paine; B. blitz; C. dwelt; D. Hoover; E. forthright; F. Kong; G. inequities; H. Delhi; I. nephew; J. fleshy; K. unity
"When men yield up the privilege of thinking, the last shadow of liberty quits the horizon."

Football Fever by Alpha Sleuth™ (page 17)

	S	W	I	F	T			Q
	M		N			R		U
	A		J			E		A
	C	L	U	B	S	C		R
	K		R		H	E		T
		P	E	N	A	L	I	Z	E	R
H	O	L	D		K	V		R
		A			E	E		
O	X	Y	G	E	N	R		

P	I	G	S	K	I	N
P	L	A	Y	O	F	F

Answers

Versatile Verbiage (page 17)
BAND

Word Jigsaw (page 18)

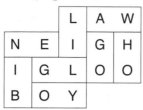

	L	A	W
N	E	I	G	H
I	G	L	O	O
B	O	Y

Word Ladder (page 18)
Answers may vary.
MICE, rice, race, rate, RATS

Can You Be Picture-Perfect? (page 19)
1. Boy in second photo has shorter hair; 2. coffee added to cup; 3. cup handle moved left; 4. fluting on neck of vase is different

Word Ladder (page 20)
Answers may vary.
TRUE, tree, free, flee, flue, BLUE

Contain Yourself (page 20)
ex(pen)sive, vau(devil)le, c(Handel)ier

Shrouded Summary (page 21)

```
B  O  R  P  H  A  N  I  N  P  L  T  K  W
H  A  H  D  I  O  T  H  W  I  H  O  P  N
E  F  K  J  D  L  S  N  R  E  G  G  R  N
N  S  Y  S  E  R  H  Y  M  T  B  F  I  P
L  T  L  H  S  O  U  T  O  T  B  H  O  W
O  E  O  N  W  E  A  E  V  A  U  A  R  H
T  I  A  I  K  I  R  I  I  A  I  N  A  K
P  I  B  D  H  T  T  L  T  C  E  G  I  K
P  H  F  I  L  H  H  H  P  S  U  A  N  V
R  N  A  R  N  Q  I  A  R  H  M  N  C  W
I  Y  L  A  R  N  E  M  C  R  P  O  N  S
O  T  L  C  A  L  V  S  N  I  B  I  O  J
R  E  G  O  J  B  E  F  O  R  E  N  G  M
A  I  A  D  L  F  S  I  I  E  K  S  T  A
I  M  L  I  T  L  T  N  N  A  N  I  N  C
Z  C  I  Y  D  N  E  D  G  L  J  L  P  A
W  Y  W  J  T  K  I  I  F  A  M  I  L  Y
F  A  P  O  S  N  C  N  B  W  N  L  E  M
I  D  L  F  N  T  R  G  U  P  R  H  A  S
H  T  R  O  T  H  E  R  T  L  S  T  D  U
T  U  A  R  D  A  I  E  G  A  N  G  E  F
D  S  I  F  G  L  F  M  A  N  I  A  R  B
N  W  R  A  T  V  W  L  D  S  D  G  D  L
```

Orphan hides out with thieves before finding real family, but gang leader has other plans for him. "Oliver Twist" by Charles Dickens

Find the Word (page 22)
Fred, **og**re of the land of Pra**do G**amma, declared that the **dog**ma of en**dog**amy, requiring him to we**d og**res only, was unfair. Fred **dog**gedly courted En**dog**ia, a lover of avoca**do g**um, but not a weir**do g**irl. He wrote her **dog**gerel, sent her hot**dog**s, and took her to a black tie dinner, but his tuxe**do g**ot caught on a nail, and everyone saw his Spee**do g**arment underneath. Fred moped in his con**do g**arage until En**dog**ia's parents, after much a**do, g**ave their permission to we**d. Og**res from Pra**do G**amma thought the wedding was a boon**dog**gle, and they were proven right when Fre**d og**led the maid of honor and En**dog**ia said, "No can **do**—goodbye!"

Name Calling (page 22)
gloves

Sudoku (page 23)

4	7	9	1	8	3	5	6	2
6	3	5	4	2	9	8	1	7
2	8	1	5	6	7	3	9	4
7	5	4	6	1	2	9	3	8
8	6	2	9	3	4	7	5	1
1	9	3	8	7	5	4	2	6
3	4	6	7	5	1	2	8	9
9	2	8	3	4	6	1	7	5
5	1	7	2	9	8	6	4	3

Three of a Kind (page 23)
1. arm/ram; 2. dub/Bud; 3. nip/pin; 4. cat/act; 5. bad/dab

Snack Attack (page 24)

Explore Your Mind (pages 26-27)

Go Figure (page 25)

						29
6	5	4	9	1	2	27
3	4	3	2	5	6	23
2	2	7	1	6	4	22
1	6	5	7	5	3	27
8	9	4	3	3	1	28
7	4	3	4	4	5	27
27	30	26	26	24	21	32

Hinky Pinky (page 25)

1. clean/green; 2. cold/gold; 3. chose/rose;
4. cite/White; 5. crown/Brown
Double theme: The first words start with the
letter C, and the second words are colors.

Animal House (page 28)

	Name	Animal	Location
1	Brenda	elephant	cave
2	Clive	goat	wood
3	Andy	horse	field
4	Dolly	flamingo	shed

Anagrams at Work (page 28)

general/enlarge

Code-Doku (page 29)

T	D	N	H	W	S	A	L	E
L	E	H	T	N	A	S	D	W
S	A	W	E	L	D	T	N	H
N	L	S	W	D	T	E	H	A
A	T	D	S	E	H	L	W	N
H	W	E	N	A	L	D	T	S
D	N	L	A	S	W	H	E	T
W	S	T	D	H	E	N	A	L
E	H	A	L	T	N	W	S	D

ALL'S WELL THAT ENDS WELL

Number Crossword (page 29)

Answers

Word Columns (page 30)

A	s		s	o	o	n		a	s		y	o	u		s	i	t		d	o	w	n
t	o		a		c	u	p		o	f		h	o	t		c	o	f	f	e	e	,
y	o	u	r		b	o	s	s		w	i	l	l		a	s	k		y	o	u
	t	o		d	o		s	o	m	e	t	h	i	n	g		w	h	i	c	h
w	i	l	l		l	a	s	t		u	n	t	i	l		t	h	e
	c	o	f	f	e	e		i	s		c	o	l	d	.

As soon as you sit down to a cup of hot coffee, your boss will ask you to do something which will last until the coffee is cold.

A Real Cakewalk (page 31)

Word Ladder (page 31)

Answers may vary.
CORK, work, wore, wire, WINE

Sudoku (page 32)

2	1	7	6	8	3	5	9	4
4	6	5	9	7	1	3	2	8
3	8	9	4	2	5	6	1	7
9	4	2	5	3	6	7	8	1
1	7	3	8	9	2	4	6	5
6	5	8	7	1	4	2	3	9
8	2	1	3	5	7	9	4	6
7	3	6	1	4	9	8	5	2
5	9	4	2	6	8	1	7	3

Fitting Words (page 32)

A	M	B	L	E
K	O	R	E	A
I	R	O	N	S
N	E	W	S	Y

Letterbox Passport (page 33)

1	2	3	4	5	6	7	8	9	10	11	12	13
G	S	W	I	T	Z	E	R	L	A	N	D	H

14	15	16	17	18	19	20	21	22	23	24	25	26
P	Y	Q	K	U	J	X	C	V	B	M	O	F

Word Jigsaw (page 34)

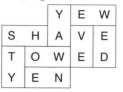

		Y	E	W
S	H	A	V	E
T	O	W	E	D
Y	E	N		

A Whale of a Challenge (page 34)

Army Show (page 35)

	Title	Surname	Act
1	Private	Buckshot	juggling
2	Major	Bark	comedy
3	Colonel	Rattle	acting
4	Sergeant	Trumpet	piano

Eight Is Enough (page 35)

downside/disowned

Acrostic Clues (page 36)

A. Ralph Waldo Emerson; B. Russia;
C. dynamite; D. washout; E. testifies;
F. Sweden; G. hibernate; H. halibut; I. twitch
"What lies behind us and what lies before us are tiny matters compared to what lies within us."

What's Wrong With This Picture? (page 37)

1. One of the essays is posted sideways; 2. there are no hands on the clock; 3. the carnival poster uses the wrong spelling of "week"; 4. the world map is labeled as a map of the United States; 5. the first math problem is wrong; 6. the teacher is a woman, so her name isn't Mr. Grimm; 7. the cabinet has a big envelope for a drawer; 8. there is a hand floating in the air; 9. desk in the front row is actually a big book; 10. the bookcase is upside down; 11. child has a balloon for a head; 12. the boy in the striped shirt is sitting without a chair; 13. whispering girl's chair is missing legs 14. boy the whispering girl is talking to has a big button for a desk; 15. boy's shirt is on backward; 16. boy throwing paper has two different shirt sleeves

Wax On, Wax Off (pages 38–39)

S	S	T	S		N	A	P	S		P	H	I
O	K	R	A		O	M	I	T		E	I	N
M	O	O	N	S	H	I	N	E		S	A	T
M	A	L	A	W	I		K	E	T	T	L	E
E	L	L		E	T	C		P	A	L	E	R
			A	L	T	A	R		P	E	A	S
	A	P	P	L	E	P	O	L	I	S	H	
D	R	O	P		R	E	A	I	R			
A	M	P	L	E		D	D	T		M	R	I
P	O	L	Y	P	S		S	H	O	O	I	N
P	I	A		I	N	T	H	E	B	U	F	F
E	R	R		C	I	A	O		I	S	L	E
R	E	S		S	T	O	W		S	E	E	R

Where We Live (page 40)

Name Calling (page 40)

words

Number Crossword (page 41)

2	4	6	
3	4	5	6
1	2	4	8
	2	3	6

Hinky Pinky (page 41)

1. quick/lick; 2. bank/prank; 3. Phillie's/lilies;
4. narrow/arrow; 5. panelists'/analysts

Sudoku (page 42)

7	2	9	6	4	1	8	5	3
5	6	8	2	7	3	9	1	4
4	1	3	5	8	9	2	6	7
6	7	4	1	5	8	3	9	2
3	5	2	9	6	7	4	8	1
8	9	1	3	2	4	5	7	6
1	3	7	8	9	2	6	4	5
2	8	6	4	1	5	7	3	9
9	4	5	7	3	6	1	2	8

Powerful Anagrams (page 42)

erupted/reputed

A Puzzling Perspective (page 43)

Neanderthal

Word Ladder (page 43)

Answers may vary.
DAILY, doily, dolly, dolls, doles, dozes, DOZEN

Gesundheit! by Alpha Sleuth™ (page 44)

COLD AND FLU

Fitting Words (page 45)

W	A	L	T	Z
A	L	O	H	A
S	T	R	A	P
P	O	E	T	S

Sucker Bet (page 45)

Shirley has been married twice to guys named Vern, and she has visited Atlantic City once with each of them. Shirley is the second Vern's first and only wife.

Answers

Holy Isograms! (page 46)

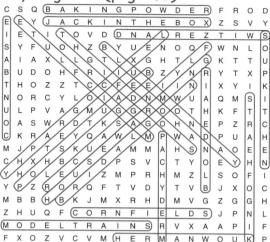

Go Figure (page 47)

					300
2	4	6	3	144
1	2	5	4	40
3	5	2	3	90
4	1	2	4	32
24	40	120	144	32

Word Jigsaw (page 47)

	G	A	S
P	O	R	C	H
U	N	I	T	Y
	B	E	D

Bad Weather (pages 48–49)

U	S	E		N	Y	P	D		V	I	N	E
P	U	G		O	A	H	U		I	R	O	N
L	I	G	H	T	N	I	N	G	B	O	L	T
A	T	T	A	C	K			E	R	N	I	E
T	O	O	T	H		A	S	S	A	Y	E	R
E	R	S			A	M	U	S	T			
			S	T	O	R	M	D	O	O	R	
			I	O	T	A	S			E	S	P
S	A	G	E	H	E	N		F	A	C	T	O
O	S	S	I	E			T	A	I	L	O	R
T	H	U	N	D	E	R	S	T	R	U	C	K
T	O	I	T		M	E	A	T		S	K	Y
O	T	T	O		S	P	R	Y		E	S	S

Take a Shot (page 50)

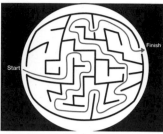

Number Square (page 50)

3	5	7
9	1	4
8	2	6

Code-Doku (page 51)

E	M	U	T	S	H	O	I	C
S	T	H	O	C	I	E	M	U
O	I	C	U	E	M	H	S	T
T	S	M	H	I	U	C	O	E
C	U	O	S	T	E	M	H	I
H	E	I	C	M	O	U	T	S
U	H	T	E	O	S	I	C	M
I	C	E	M	H	T	S	U	O
M	O	S	I	U	C	T	E	H

MUSIC SOOTHES THE COUTH, TOO

Name Calling (page 51)
Victory

What's Wrong With This Picture? (page 52)

1. "Check-Out" spelled incorrectly; 2. the bus terminal sign doesn't belong; 3. golf clubs by the door; 4. giant suitcase instead of bookshelf; 5. bottles on bookshelf; 6. license plate (with California misspelled!) running down bookshelf; 7. dog on table; 8. elephant leg instead of table leg; 9. girl has six fingers; 10. sign on bookshelf reads "K-B"; 11. librarian has one short sleeve and one long one; 12. librarian has button holes on both sides of her vest; 13. there is a giant crack in the floor; 14. boy has a sock on his hand; 15. girl's backpack has feet; 16. there's a giant saw stuck in the bookcase; 17. hands are holding the "Science Fiction" sign; 18. boy's arm isn't attached to his body

Newsroom Scramblegram (page 53)

Contain Yourself (page 53)

Ge(Nero)sity

Sudoku (page 54)

A-mazing Twists (page 54)

Word Columns (page 55)

Sometimes I lie awake at night and ask, "Where have I gone wrong?" Then a voice says to me, "This is going to take more than one night." --Charles Schultz

Go Figure (page 56)

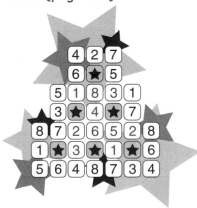

Word Ladder (page 56)

Answers may vary.
WHALE, shale, share, spare, spore, sport, SPOUT

Secret Cities? (page 57)

1. Baltimore, MD; 2. Bayonne, NJ; 3. Bowling Green, OH; 4. Boston, MA; 5. Bangor, ME; 6. Butte, MT; 7. Boise, ID; 8. Bismarck, ND; 9. Branson, MO; 10. Billings, MT; 11. Birmingham, AL

Wacky Wordy (page 57)

Neon sign (KNEE on SIGN)

Star Power (page 58)

Acrostic Clues (page 59)

A. Mahatma Gandhi; B. Neptune; C. Crete; D. fetter; E. horsepower; F. repent; G. Orthodox; H. Bonaparte; I. Loch; J. deploy; K. fight
"There are people in the world so hungry that God cannot appear to them except in the form of bread."

Answers

A Puzzling Perspective (page 60)
Grandmother

Sudoku (page 60)

4	1	9	2	3	5	7	8	6
7	6	3	4	8	1	5	9	2
2	5	8	6	7	9	1	3	4
1	3	2	8	5	7	4	6	9
9	8	6	1	4	2	3	5	7
5	7	4	9	6	3	8	2	1
3	4	1	5	9	6	2	7	8
6	2	5	7	1	8	9	4	3
8	9	7	3	2	4	6	1	5

Colorful Scramblegram (page 61)

REICES
CERISE
LS ... DM
II ... AA
VL ... MD
EV ... AK
RE ... SA
SR ... KS
SIENNA
INSANE

ERELVDNA
LAVENDER

Word Ladder (page 61)
Answers may vary.
PEAR, sear, seam, slam, slum, PLUM

Horsing Around (pages 62–63)

Red, White, and Blue (page 64)

	A	B	C	D	E	F
1	B	B	W	W	R	R
2	R	W	B	R	W	B
3	W	R	R	B	B	W
4	R	B	W	B	R	W
5	W	R	B	R	W	B
6	B	W	R	W	B	R

Word Jigsaw (page 64)

J	A	W		
E		L	I	T	E
T	E	N	O	R
		S	P	A

What's Wrong With This Picture? (page 65)

1. flap is missing on awning; 2. a fish is hanging from the plant; 3. a hat is on top of the umbrella; 4. the umbrella has no pole; 5. the sale sign is upside down; 6. the saleswoman has three arms; 7. the artist is wearing only half of a jacket; 8. a dripping hose is in with the walking sticks; 9. the dog has hooves; 10. the boy has one short pant leg; 11. the bike is missing its front wheel; 12. bottom of woman's bag is missing; 13. woman is wearing one boot and one shoe; 14. pockets on vest are upside down; 15. man is wearing swim goggles

Number Crossword (page 66)

3	3		1	6
6	5	4	3	2
	2	2	5	
9	5	3	7	1
1	3		9	7

Find the Word (page 66)

Abe **ar**ranged to meet his main ba**be**, **Ar**iel, at the fa**b ear**ring emporium in the mall. Abe applied for a jo**b ear**lier so he could **be a r**eal provider for Ariel when they wed. Ariel, a wanna**be ar**tist and a bit over**bear**ing, told **Abe a ring** wasn't enough and that she wanted matching hoop earrings, a ro**be, a r**edwood house like her fore**bear**s, and a lam**b. Ear**nest but realistic, Abe scratched his **bear**d, decided he didn't like having to ru**b ear**lobes, and quit his job. Ariel couldn't **bear** the embarrassment that the job didn't earn **Abe a r**ed cent and left him just as another ba**be, a r**edhead, caught his eye.

Make a Beeline (page 67)

K	S	O	R	K	A	Y	A	M	J	Q	L	B	T	D	T	B
Y	L	L	E	B	R	E	E	B	A	G	L	U	E	Z	S	A
J	M	L	R	E	N	R	U	B	K	C	A	B	K	B	E	T
T	R	A	I	S	P	C	T	H	X	T	B	B	N	E	U	H
R	F	D	E	B	Y	E	A	A	I	F	D	L	A	L	L	I
A	X	B	E	B	O	O	O	S	N	Q	R	E	L	T	B	N
E	O	E	E	B	E	L	B	M	U	B	A	B	B	B	Y	G
B	B	A	G	S	J	C	A	D	L	N	I	A	H	U	B	B
K	T	U	V	A	P	P	N	F	A	B	L	T	C	C	A	E
C	O	B	L	X	B	F	A	A	F	B	L	H	A	K	B	A
A	L	R	D	M	H	N	N	W	L	U	I	Q	E	L	A	U
L	L	I	B	E	L	C	A	N	R	A	B	D	B	E	N	T
B	A	D	S	E	N	O	B	E	R	A	B	U	Z	A	K	Y
D	B	G	G	N	A	B	G	I	B	E	X	V	S	Z	B	V
E	H	E	W	T	A	B	L	L	A	B	E	S	A	B	O	R
U	R	S	Z	G	S	I	I	N	I	S	A	B	T	A	O	B
B	A	R	B	E	L	L	S	B	L	U	E	B	O	O	K	Y

Fitting Words (page 68)

D	A	R	T	S
A	W	A	R	E
F	A	C	E	T
T	Y	K	E	S

See Your Way Free (page 68)

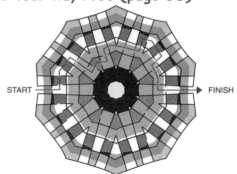

START → FINISH

Hinky Pinky (page 69)

1. jury/fury; 2. runner/shunner; 3. fervent/servant; 4. smuggest/druggist; 5. touting/scouting

Four-Thought Required (page 69)

1. last/salt; 2. spat/past; 3. ends/send; 4. mood/Doom; 5. edit/diet; 6. rued/rude; 7. rear/rare; 8. hate/heat; 9. were/ewer

Sudoku (page 70)

5	2	6	7	4	1	9	8	3
8	1	7	2	9	3	5	6	4
3	4	9	6	5	8	2	1	7
6	9	1	3	8	5	4	7	2
2	8	4	9	1	7	3	5	6
7	5	3	4	2	6	1	9	8
4	3	8	5	7	9	6	2	1
1	6	5	8	3	2	7	4	9
9	7	2	1	6	4	8	3	5

Fashionable Anagrams (page 70)

designer/resigned/redesign

Answers

Traffic Tango (page 71)

Pork Puzzler (page 72)

First place: Gomer's Berkshire
Second place: Homer's Hampshire
Third place: Romer's Duroc
Fourth place: Domer's Chester White

Word Circle (page 72)

cellar, arouse, sequel, eleven, entice

Go Figure (page 73)

					768
2	3	4	5	6	720
1	5	3	4	2	120
2	3	4	5	1	120
3	2	4	3	2	144
4	5	2	1	3	120

48 450 384 300 72 360

Hinky Pinky (page 73)

1. best/nest; 2. feed/steed; 3. Hood's/woods;
4. actor's/tractors; 5. opposing/proposing

Fruit Salad (pages 74–75)

Capital Scramblegram (page 76)

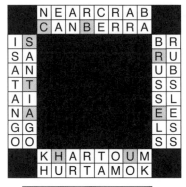

Numbers Game (page 76)

8694

Star Power (page 77)

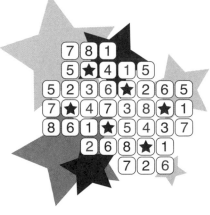

178

Find the Word (page 78)

Rufus was a kanga**roo** **f**anatic, and the **proof** was the kanga**roo f**rescoes he painted on his **roof**. Rufus owned a bist**ro, of**ten bringing home food for his pet kanga**roo**, Fido. Fido, a boxing kangaroo, was a semip**ro, of**ten fighting large wallabies. His win total was ze**ro of**ficially, although he once defeated a koala in an unofficial match when the smaller koala pulled a switche**roo**, **f**alling to throw the fight. Rufus kept Fido in a leak**proof** hut with shatter**proof** windows and read him stories of the jacka**roo**, fantastic creatures that were part rabbit and part kanga**roo**. Fido didn't believe the stories but played along because he had no **proof** and wanted Rufus to keep bringing foods from the bist**ro, of** which the rooster fondue was his favorite.

Word Jigsaw (page 78)

E	A	R		
W	R	I	T	E
E	M	B	E	R
		S	E	A

Remember Me? (pages 79-80)

seahorse, soccer ball, duck, lobster, spoon, flowers, nurse, lawnmower, hammer

More Times the Fun (page 80)

5	4	3	2 (60)	6	1
4	3	2 (48)	5	1 (15)	6
6 (144)	2	4	1	3 (225)	5
2	6	1 (30)	4 (240)	5	3
3	1	5	6	2	4
1	5	6	3	4	2

Candy's Collectibles (page 81)

The shaker on the left side of the cabinet on the second shelf from the bottom is the same as the shaker on the right side of the cabinet on the second shelf from the top

Fitting Words (page 82)

F	A	B	L	E
A	L	L	A	Y
R	O	U	S	E
M	E	E	T	S

Number Square (page 82)

9	3	6
1	7	4
2	5	8

Letterbox Aviary (page 83)

1	2	3	4	5	6	7	8	9	10	11	12	13
K	T	J	A	Y	G	P	U	C	Q	D	H	W
14	15	16	17	18	19	20	21	22	23	24	25	26
S	X	M	Z	F	R	O	B	I	N	L	V	E

Answers

A Puzzling Perspective (page 84)
Nearsighted

Code-Doku (page 84)

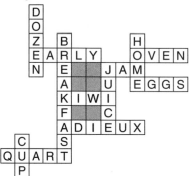

I	T	A	O	L	N	F	E	V
L	E	V	A	I	F	T	N	O
O	N	F	E	T	V	A	I	L
E	A	L	V	N	I	O	T	F
F	I	T	L	E	O	V	A	N
V	O	N	F	A	T	I	L	E
A	V	E	I	O	L	N	F	T
T	L	O	N	F	A	E	V	I
N	F	I	T	V	E	L	O	A

TALL VANILLA NONFAT LATTE

Start Your Day by Alpha Sleuth™ (page 85)

```
D
O
Z   B           H
E A R L Y       O V E N
N   E     J A M
    A     U   E G G S
    K I W I
    F     C
    A D I E U X
  C S
Q U A R T
  P
```

R I S E   A N D   S H I N E

Sudoku (page 86)

9	3	5	2	7	8	4	1	6
8	1	4	3	9	6	7	2	5
6	7	2	4	5	1	3	9	8
4	2	7	9	6	3	8	5	1
5	6	3	8	1	2	9	4	7
1	8	9	7	4	5	2	6	3
7	4	1	5	3	9	6	8	2
2	9	6	1	8	7	5	3	4
3	5	8	6	2	4	1	7	9

Desert Island Quiz (page 86)
Dean tore out page 7 and 8. There were 14 pages in the book.

Letterbox Zoo (page 87)

1	2	3	4	5	6	7	8	9	10	11	12	13
H	S	W	B	A	D	G	E	R	I	K	P	Z
14	15	16	17	18	19	20	21	22	23	24	25	26
U	M	Y	V	F	O	X	N	Q	C	J	T	L

What's Wrong With This Picture? (page 88)
1. Porthole in door, with water; 2. player is holding a tennis racket; 3. same player is missing his legs; 4. player has mismatched socks; 5. there are hopscotch lines on the court; 6. player is holding an ice cream cone; 7. same player is also holding a javelin; 8. baseboard is going through the legs of the same player; 9. that same player is wearing jeans; 10. player has knit cap on; 11. same player is also wearing an ice skate; 12. there is a foot with no player attached; 13. player shooting is wearing one high-heel shoe; 14. the basketball is actually a big tennis ball; 15. there is no net on the rim; 16. "team" is misspelled on the sign; 17. player is wearing a skirt; 18. player is wearing an oven mitt; 19. same player's uniform has different stripes from his teammates'; 20. there is a cactus on the floor

Number Crossword (page 89)

		5	1	2
	8	7	6	5
7	8		6	6
9	8	4	1	
2	8	9		

Widget Bewilderment (page 89)
Tom has 18, Dick has 24, and Harry has 32.

Merry Christmas (pages 90-91)

R	O	C	K		L	A	C	T	O		I	C	E	S
I	R	O	N		A	T	U	R	N		V	I	L	E
F	A	M	I	L	Y	T	R	E	E		Y	A	L	E
E	L	A	T	E	S		L	A	O		L	O	A	N
			S	A	A	B		T	U	N	E			
A	B	C		S	W	A	B		T	R	A	C	E	D
C	A	R	H	E	A	T	E	R		A	G	O	R	A
C	L	I	O		Y	E	S	E	S		U	L	A	N
R	E	E	L	S		S	T	A	T	U	E	T	T	E
A	D	D	L	E	S		S	C	A	T		S	O	S
			Y	W	C	A		T	G	I	F			
C	R	E	W		O	C	T		E	C	O	L	E	S
R	E	D	O		T	H	A	T	S	A	W	R	A	P
A	N	N	O		C	O	X	A	E		L	O	S	E
B	E	A	D		H	O	I	S	T		S	N	E	E

Red, White, and Blue (page 92)

	A	B	C	D	E	F
1	R	R	B	B	W	W
2	W	B	R	W	B	R
3	B	W	W	R	R	B
4	B	W	R	R	W	B
5	R	B	W	W	B	R
6	W	R	B	B	R	W

Wacky Wordy (page 92)

Frankenstein (FRANK in STEIN)

Read Between the Lines (page 93)

Figure C is next, because if you ignore the changing dots, you'll see that the figures contain the letters in the word NEWS.

Name Calling (page 93)

Colorado

Acrostic Clues (pages 94-95)

A. Leonardo da Vinci; B. daydreams; C. dived;
D. vested; E. desktop; F. fungus; G. disbands;
H. windiest; I. offensively; J. immensely
"As every divided kingdom falls, so every mind divided between many studies confounds and saps itself."

Code-Doku (page 95)

M	L	E	O	S	A	G	T	N
O	S	N	E	G	T	L	M	A
G	A	T	L	N	M	S	E	O
L	T	A	G	M	S	O	N	E
S	G	O	A	E	N	T	L	M
N	E	M	T	L	O	A	G	S
A	M	S	N	T	L	E	O	G
E	N	L	S	O	G	M	A	T
T	O	G	M	A	E	N	S	L

MOON GLEAMS ON GENTLE SEAS

A Puzzling Perspective (page 96)

Forthcoming

Fitting Words (page 96)

H	A	Z	E	L
A	S	I	D	E
R	I	N	G	S
P	A	C	E	S

Law and Disorder (page 97)

1. Paper clutter on desk replaced with a crossword puzzle; 2. the days have been stolen from the calendar; 3. spittoon is missing; 4. hole in shoe sole has been repaired; 5. sheriff's mustache is missing; 6. sheriff's badge is missing; 7. incandescent bulb in the overhead light has been replaced by a modern eco-friendly fluorescent bulb; 8. "Reward" on the poster now reads backward as "Drawer"; 9. one chair leg is gone

Intergalactic Mix-up (page 98)

	Name	Race	Planet	Galaxy
1	Evary	Florals	Nin	Q21
2	Azba	Hives	Osder	S63
3	Coot	Jollys	Mogda	R11
4	Beggle	Ginnys	Lima	T58
5	Da	Inklins	Klink	P37

Answers

Find the Word (page 99)

1. playground: Oh my, look at that **play**! **Ground** ball for sure," Beth's mom said at soft-ball practice.

2. locker: "How could this **lock er**ode inside our spaceship?" Greta asked the captain.

3. children: "I've always wanted a **child. Ren**ting one's not an option, I suppose?" asked the alien regretfully.

4. gym: "At my sleepover, we had a candy or**gy**! **M**any of us were sick the next day, too," Michael boasted proudly. "Ugh!" replied Amy.

5. teacher: Success! The doctor couldn't wait to tou**t each er**rant embryo to the whole scientific community.

6. cafeteria: "It would be an honor to ad lo**c a fete ria**lto in Venice for you, my dear," the bearded man told his latest beau in Italian. She swooned prettily and fainted in his arms.

Go Figure (page 99)

							27
6	2	1	5	3	1	5	23
1	3	6	7	4	5	2	28
6	9	4	7	1	8	1	36
2	1	8	8	3	5	9	36
4	9	2	7	5	3	3	33
6	4	3	1	5	2	7	28
2	5	5	2	1	4	9	28

27 33 29 37 22 28 36 37

Name That Scramblegram (page 100)

GREATARM — MARGARET
CARLOCOINE / REAR... — CAROLINE
SSAAMANTHAAM — SAMANTHA
KATHLEEN — THEANKLE
AECRIHTEN — CATHERINE

Sudoku (page 101)

2	7	4	3	9	6	8	1	5
9	1	3	7	8	5	4	6	2
8	5	6	1	4	2	3	7	9
5	8	9	6	1	3	2	4	7
4	6	2	8	5	7	9	3	1
1	3	7	9	2	4	6	5	8
6	2	1	4	7	9	5	8	3
7	4	5	2	3	8	1	9	6
3	9	8	5	6	1	7	2	4

Word Ladder (page 101)

Answers may vary.

BRISK, brick, crick, click, clock, BLOCK

Colorful Clues (pages 102–103)

W	O	E		D	R	E	W		S	P	O	T
H	U	T		O	A	T	H		H	O	P	E
I	C	H		Z	I	T	I		R	O	U	X
P	H	O	N	E	N	U	M	B	E	R	S	
	L	O	N				P	A	W			
Y	E	O	W		A	X	E	L		K	I	A
E	X	G	I	R	L	F	R	I	E	N	D	S
S	T	Y		E	L	L	S		L	E	S	S
			G	E	O		O	L	E			
	U	S	E	D	C	A	R	V	A	L	U	E
W	R	E	N		A	M	I	E		I	V	Y
I	S	T	O		T	E	N	N		N	E	E
N	A	S	A		E	N	D	S		G	A	S

Star Power (page 104)

A Puzzling Perspective (page 105)

Foreclosure

Word Jigsaw (page 105)

```
F E E
O R G A N
G R O P E
    S E W
```

Red, White, Blue, and Green (page 106)

	A	B	C	D	E	F	G	H
1	W	G	B	R	B	G	W	R
2	R	W	G	B	R	G	B	W
3	G	B	G	W	R	W	B	R
4	R	B	W	R	W	B	G	G
5	B	R	B	G	G	R	W	W
6	W	W	R	G	B	B	R	G
7	G	G	W	B	W	R	R	B
8	B	R	R	W	G	W	G	B

Fitting Words (page 107)

```
S H A L L
C U R I O
A G E N T
M E A T S
```

Sudoku (page 107)

```
7 2 1 5 8 9 6 3 4
6 8 4 3 7 2 5 9 1
5 9 3 6 1 4 7 8 2
4 7 5 9 2 1 8 6 3
3 1 2 8 5 6 4 7 9
8 6 9 4 3 7 1 2 5
1 4 8 7 9 3 2 5 6
2 3 7 1 6 5 9 4 8
9 5 6 2 4 8 3 1 7
```

Name Calling (page 108)

brilliant

Word Ladder (page 108)

Answers may vary.
CHIP, chop, coop, coos, cops, tops, tips, DIPS

The Upper Crust by Alpha Sleuth™ (page 109)

LIVING LARGE

Star Power (page 110)

Go Figure (page 111)

									44
7	9	6	1	5	2	4	8		42
8	9	2	8	7	6	7	8		55
3	7	4	9	8	7	6	5		49
5	6	4	9	8	7	6	5		50
5	6	7	2	8	9	9	5		51
9	5	4	5	2	8	8	7		48
7	6	3	8	7	3	4	9		47
2	4	9	1	6	5	8	7		42

46 52 39 43 51 47 52 54 56

Tasty Toss (page 111)

Pat: blueberry pies, yellow apron
Quinn: lemon pies, brown apron
Rhoda: chocolate pies, blue apron
Sam: strawberry pies, red apron

Answers

Face the Music (pages 112–113)

A Puzzling Perspective (page 114)

Retrofitted

Word Pyramid (page 114)

SEA
SANE
SNARE
RAVENS
RAVINES
INVADERS
VINEYARDS

Code-Doku (page 115)

S	N	L	T	E	A	O	I	X
O	T	I	N	L	X	E	S	A
X	A	E	I	S	O	T	N	L
I	O	S	A	N	E	X	L	T
N	L	A	X	I	T	S	O	E
T	E	X	S	O	L	I	A	N
A	I	N	E	T	S	L	X	O
L	X	T	O	A	I	N	E	S
E	S	O	L	X	N	A	T	I

NEATNESS IS NEXT TO SAINTLINESS

Animal Anagrams (page 115)

coolest/ocelots

Acrostic Clues (page 116)

A. Susan Sontag; B. Hirohito; C. campsite;
D. prevented; E. worthwhile; F. prophets;
G. chamber; H. Einstein; I. hotter; J. typhoon
"In America, the photographer is not simply the
person who records the past, but the one who
invents it."

Word Jigsaw (page 117)

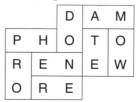

Fill 'Er Up (page 117)

1. Fill bucket A; 2. fill bucket B from bucket A,
filling B and leaving 5 gallons in A; 3. empty
bucket B; 4. refill bucket B from bucket A, this
leaves 1 gallon in bucket A; 5. empty bucket
B and put the 1 gallon from A into B; 6. refill
bucket A; 7. fill bucket B from bucket A—it will
take 3 gallons, leaving 6 gallons in A

Sudoku (page 118)

9	2	5	7	3	1	4	8	6
3	1	6	5	8	4	9	2	7
4	7	8	9	2	6	1	3	5
1	5	2	4	7	8	3	6	9
7	6	9	3	5	2	8	4	1
8	4	3	1	6	9	7	5	2
5	8	4	6	1	7	2	9	3
2	3	1	8	9	5	6	7	4
6	9	7	2	4	3	5	1	8

Make Sense of the Symbols (page 118)

Option D is next, because if you rotate each of
the symbols 90 degrees counter-clockwise, you'l
see the initial letters of the traditional 9 planets
in our solar system (before Pluto was demoted t
dwarf planet status).

Answers

Tight Quarters (page 119)

Stately Letterbox (page 120)

1	2	3	4	5	6	7	8	9	10	11	12	13
Q	J	R	A	U	V	C	L	D	X	E	S	Z
14	15	16	17	18	19	20	21	22	23	24	25	26
P	H	B	W	Y	O	M	I	N	G	F	K	T

Star Power (page 121)

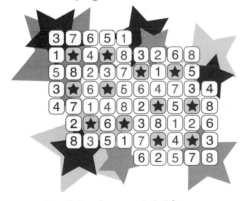

Jersey Jumble (page 122)

Dave Thom's son is Al Thom
Chuck Vance's son is Bob Vance
Ed Unger's son is Chuck Unger
Al Wolf's son is Dave Wolf
Bob Smith's son is Ed Smith

Fitting Words (page 122)

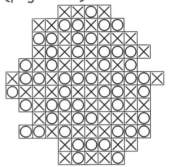

XOXO (page 123)

A Little Bit of Everything (pages 124–125)

Find the Word (page 126)

Sandwich **Andy** ran a sandwich **and y**ogurt stand that you couldn't get a seat in at lunchtime. As a youth, **Andy** planned to play pro tennis, but he had a back**hand y**ou could return handily. Andy's friend K**han dy**ed afghan dashikis for the waiters, and Margo**h, Andy**'s girlfriend, cooked soup made from matzo**h and y**ummy chicken. Sandwich **Andy** decorated his stand with cartoons from his favorite books, *Winnie the Poo**h and Y**ertle the Turtle*. Sandwich **Andy** planned to hand the stand to his friend Randy, a **handy**man who thought it was better to be disinterested **than dy**slexic. An orp**han dy**ing to understand sandwiches, Randy handled the fish **and y**ellow mustard departments and proved to be **handy**.

185

Answers

Number Crossword (page 126)

		9	1	4
	1	3	8	7
1	3		4	3
6	7	8	9	
9	7	5		

Home Office Havoc (page 127)

1. All the flowers are intact; 2. spoon is missing from bowl; 3. napkin under the bowl is different; 4. lightbulb is missing from lamp; 5. sticky note missing from computer monitor; 6. book under the lamp turned from white to black; 7. glasses turned into sunglasses; 8. sticky note removed from book on shelf; 9. bobblehead toy missing; 10. a speaker appeared next to the computer; 11. the glass is empty; 12. one of the papers is missing from the keyboard; 13. paper removed from pig picture-holder; 14. pig's eyes are looking in a different direction; 15. a different blanket is hanging on the chair; 16. ball missing from top of small monitor; 17. small monitor screen turned white; 18. scissors missing from pencil cup; 19. headphones missing from MP3 player; 20. cord on headphones is in a different position; 21. one of the videotapes is missing; 22. coffee mug has a different pattern; 23. candle is lit; 24. candleholder missing

Amusement Park by Alpha Sleuth™ (page 128)

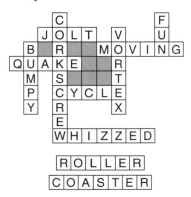

Red, White, Blue, and Green (page 129)

	A	B	C	D	E	F	G	H
1	G	B	W	R	W	R	G	B
2	R	W	B	R	G	G	B	W
3	W	G	R	G	B	W	B	R
4	G	W	R	B	G	R	W	B
5	W	B	G	W	R	B	R	G
6	B	R	G	W	R	B	W	G
7	B	R	W	G	B	W	G	R
8	R	G	B	B	W	G	R	W

Go Figure (page 130)

3	3	3	1	27
6	1	6	5	180
4	2	1	2	16
1	3	5	5	75

72 18 90 50

Word Circle (page 130)

stormy, mystic, icicle, legacy, cymbal, allure, reflex, excise, sexist

Acrostic Clues (page 131)

A. Somerset Maugham; B. Fenimore; C. flamenco D. cremation; E. fortieth; F. Robin Hood; G. affair; H. inoculating; I. confound

"I can imagine no more comfortable frame of mind for the conduct of life than a humorous resignation."

Sudoku (page 132)

9	4	3	2	1	7	5	8	6
8	2	6	5	4	3	1	7	9
1	7	5	9	8	6	4	3	2
3	5	9	7	2	4	6	1	8
4	1	2	6	5	8	7	9	3
6	8	7	3	9	1	2	4	5
5	6	4	1	3	9	8	2	7
2	3	8	4	7	5	9	6	1
7	9	1	8	6	2	3	5	4

Hinky Pinky (page 132)
1. drill/skill; 2. reach/beach; 3. faulted/malted;
4. pester/jester; 5. reoccupation/preoccupation

Word Columns (page 133)

It is rumored that Bobby Fischer got bored of playing chess with Russians. He asked the association to fix his next match with some other Europeans. It seems his telegram read, "How about a Czech mate?"

All Mixed Up (pages 134–135)

The Bicker Prize (page 136)

	Name	Surname	Book
1	Freda	Handle	Nemesis
2	Amy	Golem	Maddy
3	Cedric	Jacobs	Rodent
4	Betty	Keene	Patronage
5	Dennis	Indigo	Oasis
6	Evelyn	Lever	Quanta

Time Well Spent (page 136)
elapse/asleep/please

Star Power (page 137)

Code-Doku (page 138)

ONE SMALL STEP ON A PALE MOON

A Puzzling Perspective (page 138)
Proprietary

Alien Revolution (page 139)

Rotate each inner circle 90 degrees counter-clockwise so the lines in the inner and outer circles form the letters U, F, O, and S.

Word Ladder (page 139)
Answers may vary.
HITCH, witch, wince, since, singe, sings, wings, wines, wives, hives, hikes, HIKER

Trick or Treat! by Alpha Sleuth™ (page 140)

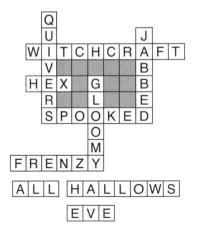

Answers

Number Crossword (page 141)

7	5	6	
2	3	4	1
	1	2	5	8
	8	6	4

Wacky Wordy (page 141)

Father-in-law (DAD inside of JUDGE)

Sudoku (page 142)

9	7	3	6	2	5	8	1	4
2	6	4	8	3	1	7	5	9
8	5	1	7	9	4	6	3	2
6	8	5	3	1	2	4	9	7
3	9	7	4	6	8	1	2	5
4	1	2	9	5	7	3	8	6
5	3	9	1	4	6	2	7	8
1	4	8	2	7	9	5	6	3
7	2	6	5	8	3	9	4	1

Birthday Party Puzzle (page 142)

Steve's daughter is 5-year-old Alicia; Larry's daughter is 6-year-old Brianna; Jeff's daughter is 7-year-old Carol; Tom's daughter is 8-year-old Darla

Keep 'Em Separated (page 143)

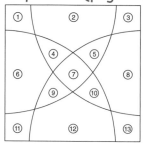

Red, White, Blue, and Green (page 144)

	A	B	C	D	E	F	G	H
1	G	R	W	R	W	G	B	B
2	R	W	B	G	R	G	B	W
3	B	R	W	B	G	W	R	G
4	G	B	R	B	W	R	W	G
5	W	B	G	R	B	W	G	R
6	B	G	G	W	B	R	R	W
7	W	G	R	W	R	B	G	B
8	R	W	B	G	G	B	W	R

Word Ladder (page 145)

Answers may vary.
WHEAT, cheat, cleat, bleat, bloat, float, flout, FLOUR

A Puzzling Perspective (page 145)

Elephantine

Manly Names (pages 146–147)

J	A	Y	W	A	L	K		F	I	R	T	H
I	N	E	R	T	I	A		A	L	O	H	A
B	O	L	I	V	A	R		X	E	B	E	C
E	S	P	N		T	A	P	E	D	E	C	K
D	E	S	K	S		T	Y	S		S	E	N
		L	A	U	E	R		S	O	L	E	
U	N	G	E	N	T	L	E	M	A	N	L	Y
P	E	A	S		T	E	X	A	N			
T	O	M		P	E	S		J	A	B	B	A
O	N	E	H	O	R	S	E		T	A	L	L
P	A	T	E	R		O	R	D	I	N	A	L
A	T	E	A	T		N	I	R	V	A	N	A
R	E	S	T	S		S	Q	U	E	L	C	H

Code-Doku (page 148)

B	U	S	Y	O	K	R	C	A
R	Y	A	C	B	S	K	O	U
C	K	O	U	R	A	B	Y	S
O	B	K	A	S	C	U	R	Y
U	R	C	O	Y	B	S	A	K
S	A	Y	R	K	U	O	B	C
K	O	U	B	A	Y	C	S	R
Y	S	B	K	C	R	A	U	O
A	C	R	S	U	O	Y	K	B

BUSY CRABS SCURRY BY ROCKY BAY

XX Marks This Spot (page 148)

4: each group of 3 numbers totals 20

Fitting Words (page 149)

G	R	I	S	T
A	U	D	I	O
W	I	L	T	S
K	N	E	E	S

Hinky Pinky (page 149)

1. annual/manual; 2. detention/pretension;
3. latitude/gratitude; 4. mutiny/scrutiny;
5. lawbreaker's/jawbreakers

Answers

Acrostic Clues (page 150)

A. Will Rogers; B. abdicated; C. Styx;
D. weeded; E. neophyte; F. shotgun;
G. elucidated; H. Stephen; I. venture; J. honey
"I never expected to see the day when girls
would get sunburned in the places they do
today."

Word Jigsaw (page 151)

	A	P	E		
C	A	C	T	I	
E	T	H	E	R	
		O	A	K	

Number Noggin-Scratcher (pages 151–152)

B. 975

Number Crossword (page 152)

			7	2	9
	6	5	4	3	
1	2	1	4	8	
8	1	9	2		
6	9	3			

Star Power (page 153)

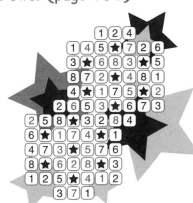

Scramblegram U.S. Tour (page 154)

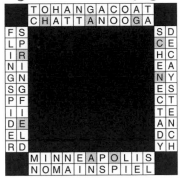

Sudoku (page 155)

9	1	5	7	3	2	8	6	4
6	3	7	4	9	8	5	2	1
2	8	4	6	5	1	9	3	7
1	9	3	2	8	6	7	4	5
7	5	6	9	4	3	2	1	8
4	2	8	5	1	7	3	9	6
5	7	9	1	2	4	6	8	3
8	6	1	3	7	9	4	5	2
3	4	2	8	6	5	1	7	9

Stadium Improvements (page 155)

spread/Padres/spared/drapes

Word Columns (page 156)

189

Answers

Get It Straight (page 157)

Mail Service (pages 158-159)

F	I	N	A	G	L	E		S	A	B	R	A
A	S	I	S	A	I	D		A	T	E	U	P
C	A	T	S	P	A	W		R	I	A	N	T
T	A	R	A		R	A	N	G	T	R	U	E
S	C	O	U	T		R	O	E		C	P	R
		L	A	U	D	S		D	U	T	Y	
P	O	S	T	O	F	F	I	C	E	B	O	X
A	C	T	S		F	U	R	O	R			
C	A	R		F	D	R		D	I	C	E	D
I	N	I	T	I	A	L	S		S	O	L	O
F	A	K	E	S		O	P	T	I	M	A	L
I	D	E	S	T		N	A	I	V	E	T	E
C	A	S	T	S		G	R	E	E	T	E	D

Word Ladder (page 160)

Answers may vary.

CEDAR, ceder, cedes, codes, cores, corps, coops, chops, chows, chews, chess, CHEST

Rounders (page 160)

Figure A is the odd one out because the other 4 figures have both concave and convex parts.

Name Calling (page 161)

Impossible

Memory Mishmash (pages 161-162)

1. There are 3 white circles in the grid; 2. N is beneath the triangle; 3. the arrow is pointing to the square; 4. the music note symbol appears in the top left-hand corner; 5. there are 3 black circles in the grid; 6. the T is to the right of a white circle; 7. R is the letter in the second row

Fitting Words (page 162)

K	A	R	M	A
E	Q	U	I	P
G	U	I	L	E
S	A	N	D	S

Creature Feature by Alpha Sleuth™ (page 163)

Strings Attached (page 164)

SCARLET CAD/CAT'S CRADLE; SOPHIE FLING/FISHING POLE; TRAINEE TOM/MARIONETTE; ANCIENT TREKS/TENNIS RACKET; TOE BOIL/BOLO TIE; BLIMP LUNE/PLUMB LINE; DAMN LION/MANDOLIN

Get It Straight (page 165)

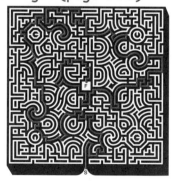

Red, White, Blue, and Green (page 166)

	A	B	C	D	E	F	G	H
1	G	W	R	G	R	W	B	B
2	W	G	W	B	B	G	R	R
3	B	B	R	G	R	W	W	G
4	R	R	B	W	B	G	W	G
5	B	W	G	R	W	R	G	B
6	R	R	W	B	G	B	G	W
7	W	G	B	R	G	R	B	W
8	G	B	G	W	W	B	R	R